IBROX Stadium, home of the mighty Glasgow Rangers, champions of Scotland for the fifth successive time. They only lost three matches last season scoring over 100 goals in the process.

The Ibrox dressing rooms whose marble and wood interior lend them an air of luxury and grandeur.

Rangers' fans in celebratory mood. They got used to that. Their idols were unbeaten at home all season.

Rangers' record last season was second to none — a domestic clean sweep and a glorious run in the European Champions' League. Can we see them next season go one better — and lift the European Cup?

£4.35

The Topical Times FOOTBALL BOOK

CON

TENTS

HAVING captained the England national side, played in European competition with Aston Villa and spent two years in the Italian League, David Platt has played alongside and against some of the world's top players.

The 27-year-old midfield star moved from Villa to Bari in the summer of 1991 and, following a subsequent transfer to Juventus, has just completed his first season with the giants of Turin.

Along with Paul Gascoigne and Des Walker, Platt has been a member of the triumvirate of players from the England team who have been starring in Italian football, and he admits that his own game has improved immensely since going to that country.

He says, "It has to be the best league in the world. Every week, whoever we play against, I'm facing top international players from a variety of countries.

"That's what makes the Italian League that bit tougher than our own league at home.

"In England, we don't have the 'great' foreigners playing in our domestic game. In Italy, however, they not only have the best of their own players playing in Serie A, the top division, but they also have the best of the foreign players. That means you'll find many of the best players in the world operating in Italy."

Nevertheless, David's list of most difficult opponents still includes a number of players with whom he shared some memorable battles in English football before going abroad.

"One of the toughest adversaries I've come up against is an England team-mate — David Batty of Leeds United.

"I always found it difficult to play against him. David is a tremendous player — tenacious and a very hard tackler.

"I once played against him while I was with Aston Villa and he'd been given the job of man-marking me. He stuck to the job well, and I never got a look in. I hardly had a touch of the ball for 90 minutes.

"Former England skipper Bryan Robson was also a tremendous opponent to come up against. Bryan was so hard to deal with because he covered so much ground that he took you into areas where you didn't want to go.

"He made his runs forward, then just as quickly got back into his own area.

"I had some tremendous battles with Robbo because that's my game as well. Whenever we were in opposition, they always turned out to be very difficult games.

"Arsenal defender Tony Adams was another who never gave you much change. It would be difficult to find a player who could beat Tony for his commitment to the game.

"You could always depend on Tony to keep his concentration for ninety minutes and remain strong against you.

Italian football is the best in the world, according to DAVID PLATT.

LEAGUE

"The hardest opponent to play against in English football, however, was Des Walker, before his move from Nottingham Forest to Sampdoria.

"If you gave Des a job to do, he always did it. For instance, if his brief was to mark a particular opponent out of the game, that's exactly what would happen.

"When I played for Villa, Tony Daley was probably the quickest player we ever had, but he never got any change out of Des.

"In terms of pace, vision . . . just about everything — Des had it all.

"Fortunately, I was never in direct opposition to Des, but any time I moved up into his penalty area, he was always a difficult player to get past."

Following his move to Italy, of course, Platt had to get used to a whole new set of tough opponents.

He goes on, "Before I actually arrived, it was difficult to know what to expect, but there were six players already in Italy whom I knew would probably be among the best I would encounter.

"They were the three German stars at Inter Milan — Lothar Mattheus, Andreas Brehme and Jurgen Klinsmann — and the three Dutchmen at AC Milan — Ruud Gullit, Marco Van Basten and Frank Rijkaard.

"Those two clubs had probably the best teams in Italy at the time. They seemed to be going for the Championship all the time, and their foreign stars were very high profile.

"I'd also come up against the three Germans already. Mattheus had made the biggest impression on me when I played for Villa against Inter in the UEFA Cup the previous season. He was such a dynamic force.

"But I also played again them in the 1990 World Cup semi-final between England and West Germany, when we lost in that dramatic penalty shoot-out.

"Again, Mattheus was the big star. He was voted the player of the tournament, an award which was well deserved.

"When I arrived in Italy, and came up against the trio again, they lived up to my expectations, although the Germans didn't figure in the Inter side during my second season.

"The three Dutchmen had just as great a reputation, having made their names in the Holland team which won the European Championship in 1988. Gullit and Van Basten have probably been lauded most, having played together up front in that side, and they have continued to justify their publicity.

Marco Van Basten

"I've been particularly impressed with Van Basten. For the past few years, I believe he has been the top centre forward in the game.

"But Rijkaard also belongs in the 'best in the game' category. He has been one of the most difficult opponents I have faced in Italy, though he doesn't enjoy the same amount of publicity, probably because he doesn't play up front like the other two. He doesn't get the credit he really deserves.

"I also rate Paolo Maldini of AC Milan very highly, but for me the best player in Italy at the moment is his clubmate, Franco Baresi.

"He is never stretched. Run at him and he always seems to have an extra second to tackle you. On the ball, he invariably has an extra yard of space to use it. Whatever is happening, Franco always seems to be playing well within himself."

According to Platt, one player belongs in the list of top players in both England and Italy — his England team-mate, Des Walker.

"Moving to Sampdoria was good for Des. His game is probably more suited to the Italian League than the English Premier League.

"However, it took a while for Des and Sampdoria to adjust to each other. His team-mate, Italian international Pietro Vierchowod, is a very similar type of player. He is quick and likes to mark people.

"However, many Italian teams play with one centre forward, so it caused problems when they had two centre halves wanting to mark the same man.

"For a spell, Des was played out of position at left back, but later Sampdoria began to operate with a sweeper, Des and Pietro lined up alongside each other, and he began to do very, very well."

LEADERS!

TEN OF THE BEST

ALL goalscorers will tell you that every goal they score is memorable. After all, there's no such thing as a bad goal.

But Manchester United and Wales striker Mark Hughes can lay claim to scoring more spectacular and crucial goals than most other Premier League hot-shots.

He's found the net during two spells at United, in Germany for Bayern Munich and in Spain for Barcelona. He's also scored many times for Wales.

Here, Mark recalls his ten most memorable goals during his ten-year career. The list is in chronological order.

May 2, 1984, Wrexham. (Home International Championships).
WALES 1, ENGLAND 0.

1 I made my international debut for Wales in this game and to score the only goal against England was a dream come true. The game was played in my home town, which made the occasion even more memorable. The goal itself wasn't one of my best. A free kick was floated into the box and I managed to get my head to the ball.

March 23, 1985, Old Trafford. (First Division).
MANCHESTER UNITED 4, ASTON VILLA 0.

2 I scored a hat-trick in this game. Although I'd scored three against Burnley in the League Cup, this was my first hat-trick in the league. The goal which completed my hat-trick stands out. When the ball came across, I found myself at the near post. I controlled the ball and flicked it over my shoulder into the far corner of the net.

April 30, 1985, Wrexham. (World Cup qualifier).
WALES 3, SPAIN 0.

3 This goal gave me a lot of recognition. We had to beat Spain to keep on course for the 1986 World Cup Finals. When the ball came to me in the air I met it on the volley and it flew into the net from 25 yards.

May 3, 1988, Bayern Munich. (Bundesliga).
BAYERN MUNICH 5, Vfl BOCHUM 0.

4 I scored only one hat-trick for Bayern Munich during my brief spell in Germany. It was against Bochum, who may not be one of the more glamorous German clubs but are a tough team to beat. For one of the goals I won a tackle outside the box and blasted the ball into the net from 20 yards.

September 23, 1989, Maine Road. (First Division).
MANCHESTER CITY 5, MANCHESTER UNITED 1.

5 My goal is the only thing I care to remember from this game. A looping cross came in from Russell Beardsmore which gave me a lot of time to think about my shot. I hit the ball with my right foot and volleyed it into the roof of the net.

May 12, 1990, Wembley. F.A. Cup Final.
MANCHESTER UNITED 3, CRYSTAL PALACE 3. (after extra time).

6 I'd scored in the second-half to give us a 2-1 lead. Ian Wright came off the bench to score either side of extra-time for Palace. We were still trailing with just nine minutes to go when I picked up a pass from Danny Wallace and struck the ball just inside the far post. We won the replay 1-0.

May 15, 1991, Rotterdam. (European Cup Winners' Cup Final).
MANCHESTER UNITED 2, BARCELONA 1.

7 I scored both the goals. The second was the best. Everyone thought I'd taken it too wide when I went round the goalkeeper and found myself faced with an acute angle. I hit it perfectly and was delighted to see it squeeze between the posts. Although I used to play for Barcelona, I didn't feel as if I was trying to make a point.

December 6, 1992, Old Trafford. (Premier League).
MANCHESTER UNITED 2, MANCHESTER CITY 1.

8 Eric Cantona made his debut for United. He marked the occasion by setting up the second for me. He knocked the ball down to me and I hit a swerving, dipping left-foot volley from just outside the penalty area into the net.

January 27, 1993, Old Trafford.
MANCHESTER UNITED 2, NOTTINGHAM FOREST 0.

9 Eric Cantona chipped in a cross to the edge of the penalty area. The ball bounced once before I whacked it into the roof of the net.

Colorsport

April 21, 1993. Selhurst Park. (Premier League).
CRYSTAL PALACE 0, MANCHESTER UNITED 2.

10 An Eric Cantona cross was volleyed into the corner of the net. The goal was entirely unexpected because I thought I was offside. Anyway, it gave us the lead and that win, coupled with Aston Villa losing 3-0 at Blackburn the same night, turned things in our favour. It was also the hundredth league goal of my career.

BRIAN O'NEILL
Celtic

DAVID KELLY
Wolves

AUCT SAL

Blackburn and Derby were the bidders preferred the First Division rather than th

DERBY COUNTY defender Craig Short knows what it's like to be the rope at the centre of a tug-of-war. The 25-year-old, who was with First Division Notts County at the time, was being pulled both ways by two clubs with the financial clout to make them the biggest spenders in the country.

Derby and Blackburn Rovers, owned by multi-millonaires Lionel Pickering and Jack Walker respectively, had put Short top of their shopping list and the price was to be no obstacle.

In the end the matter was decided by Short himself. And, ironically, it was over something which money could do nothing about.

Short had been signed by Notts County from Scarborough for just £100,000 in July 1989. He had played a key role in the Magpies' consecutive promotion campaigns which had led them to the First Division two years ago.

But relegation forced County to reluctantly put Short up for sale. Several Premier league clubs were early bidders, but dropped out as Short's price soared past the £1.5m mark.

Notts County chairman, Derek Pavis, then rubbed his hands in glee as Derby and Blackburn locked horns and pushed the fee to a record £2.5m for a defender in this country.

It was a whirlwind few weeks for Short. And he recalls that it's an experience he's never likely to forget.

"I reckon I was overpriced by a million," admits Craig. "I thought I'd go for about the same as my old County team-mate Tommy Johnson, who signed for Derby for £1.4m.

"The bidding had gone on for ages and both clubs had actually offered the same price.

"The chairman had told me to go to Derby and there was no need to speak to Blackburn. My boss, Neil Warnock, said there was only one place to go — Ewood Park!

"I wanted to make up my own mind and wanted to hear what both clubs had to offer.

"At first I had my heart set on joining Blackburn. But I talked to Derby boss, Arthur Cox, on the Sunday night and was impressed with what he had to say.

"The following morning, I drove to Blackburn and met Kenny Dalglish and Ray Harford. They made me feel very welcome.

"I asked for a couple of days to think their offer over and drove back to Nottingham. When I got home I received a phone call from Arthur Cox who asked me to go over for another chat.

"The following day, Tuesday, Kenny phoned me and said he'd left a couple of tickets for me for that night's home match against Everton. I told him I'd travel up and sign.

"As the day wore on, I began to have second thoughts. Derby seemed to be as ambitious as Blackburn, though they weren't in the Premier League, and I've grown to like living in the Midlands.

"But my wife, Joanne, and I had packed our bags and had them stacked in the hall waiting to be put in the car for the journey north. It was then that I made up my mind to go to Derby!

"I just didn't feel excited enough about going to Blackburn. I've made my reputation in the Midlands and don't feel I have to prove myself here.

"I unpacked and phoned Blackburn to tell Kenny I'd made my decision. He was in the dressing room attending to the players and was unavailable. I spoke to the chairman, who took my message and wished me luck.

"After the game, Kenny phoned and tried to persuade me to change my mind. He asked me to sleep on it and let him know in the morning. I rang back on Wednesday and confirmed I was going to Derby.

"Although he was disappointed to lose out, Kenny was very understanding and I found him to be very relaxed and quite humorous about it.

ION E!

ut Craig Short 'remier League!

"I felt terrible about making the decision and thought I'd let Blackburn down.

"If only one club was in the running, I'd probably have gone for around £1.5m. But the Notts County chairman did some good business and was able to stretch it out. I don't think £2.5m was a realistic price.

"The price tag isn't something I'm very proud of. I know some people will compare me to the price, and on the way I performed for a lot of last season I'll admit to falling short of that valuation.

"Arthur Cox told me when I signed that I shouldn't worry about the fee. He told me he wasn't expecting miracles, as long as I was a consistent performer.

"I know a lot of players let their price prey on their mind and suffer for it. I've not allowed the price to get to me too much. I have to admit, though, it certainly hasn't done me any favours.

"I had played only 40-odd games in the old First Division and had never been capped for my country. I'm sure a lot of people had never even heard of me.

"In fact, whenever I drive outside the Nottingham or Derby area in my sponsored car, I can see people waiting at traffic lights, pointing to my name on the car's side, and saying 'Craig Short? Who's he?' '

Craig explains that the decision to sign for Derby came as a big surprise to his parents. In fact, his dad had already made an investment in the belief that his son would be gracing the Premier League.

"My dad couldn't believe it when I told him," he adds. "He'd bought Sky TV because he figured he could watch me in the Premier League.

"I was a little upset because even though my dad didn't want to sound disappointed on the phone, I knew he was.

"My mum also wanted me to sign for Blackburn because she fancies Kenny Dalglish," Craig jokes.

THE MAN IN THE MIDDLE!

(A DAY IN THE LIFE OF A MAN IN BLACK)

Tuesday, March 9th, 1993 . . . Jim's day starts at breakfast with wife Anne, daughter Julie, 14, and son Scott, 9.

After a goodbye kiss from Anne, Jim leaves his detached house in Stewarton, Ayrshire, for the short drive to Lugton where he has his own contracting business.

Straightaway it's down to work. Here he discusses plans with site agent David Fleming.

After a quick snack for lunch it's time for some paperwork — bookwork of ANOTHER kind!

At the end of a busy day, Jim prepares for his next assignment — the Premier League clash between Hibs and Aberdeen at Easter Road. Jim clocks up over 2000 miles a year on his refereeing duties, so it's a fairly routine drive east to Edinburgh.

It's a game vital to both sides with Aberdeen pushing for the championship and Hibs battling for a place in Europe. Hibs' Keith Wright tries to impress on Jim his nerves of steel.

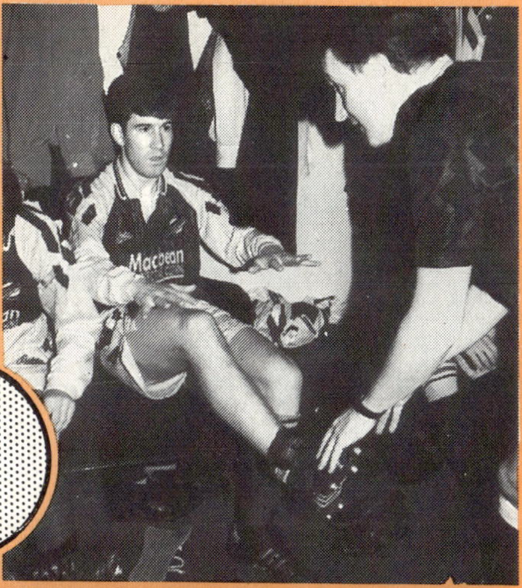

Jim leads his linesmen onto the pitch. There are 7,031 fans out there and he knows he'll be unpopular with some of them!

The match gets underway. Tension runs high and Jim is forced to wield his yellow card — five times in all!

The referee's word is final. That's the point Jim is obviously trying to impress on Hibs keeper John Burridge.

Jim McCluskey has been a grade one referee for nine years. He's had his fair share of criticism over the years but he doesn't worry. It's all part of the job. That's why he's one of Scotland's top international referees.

Full-time, the end of a hectic 90 minutes. Two goals in the last ten minutes send Aberdeen home with a 2-1 victory.

It's been a long day. Jim heads for home in Ayrshire content with his night's work. He knows he can now forget about football . . . until Saturday, that is, when another Premier League clash is on the horizon.

JUSTIN EDINBURGH
Tottenham Hotspur

MIKE NEWELL
Blackburn Rovers

SPAIN WAS OKAY, IT'S

says Aston Villa's Dalian Atkinson.

WHEN I first joined Real Sociedad, I didn't understand Spain at all. For example, when you train in England, you don't go into 50-50 challenges wanting to win the ball at all costs. You don't steam in on your team-mates.

However, the Spaniards have a different attitude. During training with Sociedad, there was a ball between me and this young lad. I went to tap it but he whacked right through it.

He went in so hard my ankle twisted right round. It was such a bad twist, I thought it was broken at the time. That injury kept me out for about two months.

Overall, however, I enjoyed Spain. I was at Sociedad at the same time as John Aldridge, the Tranmere striker, and Kevin Richardson, who is now my captain at Villa. We had some good times.

The way the locals treat you is fabulous, though it can sometimes be a bit much. If you go out in England you don't have people mobbing you for an autograph. But in Spain, you could be sitting in a restaurant and they'd all crowd round you.

And as soon as you sign

BUT...
GOOD TO BE HOME

one, that's it — you're there for hours! Once they know you're there they come in in big groups just to see you. Even a trip to the local shop to buy a tube of toothpaste takes a couple of hours!

They also tell you how you played the previous Saturday. In fact, they'll tell you what's wrong with your whole game! Everyone there is so crazy about football.

I was amazed to see my Spanish team-mates shaking at just the thought of playing in Real Madrid's Bernabeu Stadium and Barcelona's Nou Camp. We British lads wondered what was wrong with them.

We had to tell them to just go out and enjoy the atmosphere. We led them, and as soon as they realised we were having a go, they did too. In the end Sociedad won at both grounds.

When I go to Anfield in Liverpool I get a buzz from playing at such a famous stadium. As soon as I get on the pitch I try to enjoy myself as much as I can. In Spain I had the same attitude. The only difference between Anfield and the Nou Camp is the size of the crowd.

I didn't feel as if there was any pressure on me at all in Spain. The country is so laid back. They try to put everything off until tomorrow.

They thought I was a daft Englishman because I wanted things done straight away. For example, I had just moved into a new flat, but had no chairs, so I went to buy a suite from a furniture store.

I wanted to pay immediately and asked them to deliver it. The guy told me I could pay for it the next day and he'd do it then. I explained that I was in an apartment with no chairs, only lived up the road and would pay on the spot. But he said the deliveryman only came in when he felt like it! I waited ages for that couch!

And San Sebastian, where I lived, is a Basque part of Spain. The Basques consider themselves better than other Spaniards and want to have their own government. They can get quite fanatical about it.

Once, I was about to leave the club wearing a yellow T-shirt with bits of red on it. I was stopped by one of the Sociedad players and told not to go out wearing it because the locals might get upset.

I was disappointed because I think I look good in yellow, so I wanted to know why. He told me that because red and yellow are the colours of the Spanish flag the Basques wouldn't like it and they might beat me up . . . I changed the shirt!

But despite all that, Spain was a nice experience. However, it was great to get back. When offered the chance to play for Villa I couldn't turn it down. I had offers from other Spanish clubs, but I wanted to come home.

When I finally stepped off the plane in England I was so glad to be back I shouted: YES!

Tranmere's free-scoring John Aldridge — a team-mate of Dalian's at Real Sociedad.

IAN DURRANT
Rangers

KERRY DIXON
Southampton

SPECIAL COMPLETE STORY
STAR PUPIL
Tommy Janvers was Melville Town's captain and midfield general, a man dedicated to the finer aspects of the game . . .
GET FORWARD THEN! FAR POST! MOVE!
THAT'S BRILLIANT! DID IT WITHOUT THINKING!
DIDN'T SEEM TO BE LOOKING, EITHER. TOMMY'S A NATURAL!
An inch-perfect cross to striker Barry Hudson —
THE SKIPPER DOES IT EVERY TIME. RIGHT ON MY NUT. THAT'S GOT TO GO IN!
YOU WERE PUSHING, HUDSON! YOU'D GET BOOKED FOR THAT IN A MATCH.
RUBBISH! GREAT HEADER! CAN'T MISS 'EM WHEN TOMMY KNOCKS 'EM ACROSS LIKE THAT.
Later —
COULD I HAVE A WORD, TOMMY?
HANG ABOUT, BRIAN . . .
IS THAT YOU, GINO? TOMMY JANVERS HERE. COULD YOU SEND A PIZZA ROUND TO MY FLAT THIS EVENING? I'LL BE THERE ABOUT SEVEN. YEAH, ONE OF YOUR SPECIALS . . . I'M HUNGRY . . .
Brian Grant was one of Melville Town's promising youngsters.
YOU SAID YOU'D GIVE ME SOME COACHING TOMORROW. THAT STILL ON?
SURE! TEN O'CLOCK. I'LL BE THERE, BRIAN — SO DON'T BE LATE!
And so, next day —
DON'T LOB IT ACROSS LIKE THAT! THAT'S A PASS THAT WILL GO NOWHERE . . .
A DEFENDER WILL CUT THAT OUT EVERY TIME . . . JUST LIKE THIS! IT'S IN THE AIR TOO LONG.

THIRTY-YARD PASSES GO WRONG NINE TIMES OUT OF TEN. KEEP 'EM SHORT! HIT 'EM TEN YARDS . . . HARD AND LOW. LIKE THIS! UNDERSTAND?
YEAH! I SUPPOSE SO!
A couple of hours later —
I'VE HAD IT, TOMMY. CAN I GO NOW?
HALF AN HOUR YET. COME ON, CATCH UP . . . GET THOSE LEGS MOVING.
Brian's personal training continued on Wednesday evening —
SORRY I'M LATE, TOMMY . . .
I DON'T WANT TO KNOW ABOUT BEING LATE, SON. YOU BE HERE WHEN I TELL YOU!
WATCH THE BALL! DON'T WATCH MY FEET! YOU'LL NEVER GET THE BALL UNLESS YOU LOOK AT IT. AM I GETTING THROUGH TO YOU?
SORRY! I THOUGHT I HAD IT THAT TIME . . .
DON'T LOOK SO MISERABLE! YOU'RE DOING OKAY. YOU'RE GETTING GOOD RESULTS WITH THE RESERVES. YOU'LL MAKE IT.
ONE DAY, PERHAPS. BUT I NEVER SEEM TO DO ANYTHING RIGHT. YOU'RE ALWAYS GETTING ON AT ME, TOO . . .
I KEEP NAGGING YOU BECAUSE YOU'VE GOT TALENT. BUT YOU'VE GOT TO WORK. ONE DAY, YOU'LL THANK ME FOR IT.
Saturday, Melville Town v. Lester City —
THAT'S YOURS, TOMMY!
KEEP IT IN PLAY, TOMMY, SON!
ARHHHH!
WOW! SOME TACKLE! TOMMY'S HURT!
Manager Willie Grant —
IT LOOKS BAD, BOSS. I THINK IT'S BROKEN!
GO WITH THE AMBULANCE TO THE HOSPITAL, MIKE. LET'S HOPE IT'S NOT AS BAD AS IT LOOKS!
In the boardroom after the match —
SO, THEY'RE PUTTING JANVERS' LEG IN PLASTER. WHAT DO WE DO ABOUT THE CUP-TIE NEXT WEEK?
TOMMY'S BEEN COACHING BRIAN GRANT. HE RECKONS THE KID'S GOOD.
OKAY, WE'LL PLAY GRANT. WE'LL FIND OUT JUST HOW GOOD HE REALLY IS!

F.A. Cup . . . Melville v. Blackmoor —
TOWN TOWN MELVILLE TOWN!
GET USED TO IT, SON. YOU'LL HEAR IT FOR THE NEXT NINETY MINUTES!
I'M ON MY OWN, NOW. NO TOMMY TO KEEP ON AT ME, TO KEEP ME RIGHT.
TOWN! TOWN! COME ON TOWN!
TAKE IT UP, BRIAN . . . PLENTY OF TIME!
I'LL GET RID OF IT! BEFORE I LOSE IT . . .
WHAT SORT OF PASS IS THAT? I'M NOT TEN FEET TALL! I'LL NEVER GET TO THAT SORT OF BALL!
Ten minutes later —
WAKEN UP, GRANT! YOU'RE SUPPOSED TO STOP HIM!
USELESS! DUNNO WHY THEY PLAYED HIM!
Half-time, nil-nil —
PHONE CALL FOR YOU, SON. I HOPE IT'S NOT YOUR GIRL-FRIEND!
FOR ME? NO. I HAVEN'T GOT A GIRL-FRIEND. WONDER WHO IT IS?
Tommy was watching the match live on TV —
BACK TO THE BIG MATCH AT MELVILLE TOWN'S STADIUM FOR THE SECOND HALF . . .
BRIAN? LISTEN! I'VE BEEN WATCHING YOU ON TV. HAVE YOU FORGOTTEN EVERYTHING I'VE TAUGHT YOU? USE TEN YARD PASSES! WATCH THE BALL! CONCENTRATE!
OUT YOU GO, LADS . . .
YOU KNOW HOW TO PLAY. YOU CAN DO IT! NOW, GET YOUR HEAD UP. DO IT THE WAY I'VE TOLD YOU!
YEAH! OKAY, TOMMY . . . THANKS FOR THE CALL!
And so —
GOOD TACKLE! THE KID'S GOT IT!
THAT'S A GOOD BALL! HE'S PUT STEVENS AWAY!
THAT'S MORE LIKE IT, SON!

Ten minutes to go —
BRIAN GRANT AGAIN! GOOD RUN!
THE KID'S DOING BETTER!
TOMMY WAS ON THE PHONE . . . GAVE HIM A RIGHT ROASTING!
GET IT IN THE MIDDLE, SON!
NICE CROSS! KEVIN JACKSON'S GOING FOR IT!
IT'S THERE! KEVIN JACKSON! HE'S SCORED! WHAT A GOAL!
Melville Town won one-nil —
BRILLIANT STUFF! WE TURNED 'EM OVER IN THE SECOND HALF!
WE'LL WIN THE CUP IF WE KEEP PLAYING LIKE THAT!
FANCY TOMMY JANVERS PHONING! GETTING ON AT ME IN THE MIDDLE OF A MATCH. NAGGING ME . . .
WORKED THOUGH, DIDN'T IT? I PLAYED A BLINDER!
THE END

WHEN you have suffered the experience of being an outsider attempting to prove yourself a worthy paid-up member of the notorious Wimbledon 'Crazy Gang' like I did, becoming the country's most expensive full-back is nothing in comparison.

Last season, I made the move from the London outfit to Manchester City for £2.5 million. But the pressure of wearing that price tag at a big club like City just doesn't compare to the first six months I spent at Wimbledon. That was what I call pressure!

Being accepted by the infamous bunch led by the likes of John Fashanu, Vinny Jones and Dennis Wise in the late eighties was a much tougher proposition than anything the critics might have cared to throw in my direction when I made my headline-making record switch to Maine Road.

I moved to Plough Lane in 1987 when the then manager Bobby Gould paid £100,000 to Swansea City for me. I was bought to replace crowd favourite Nigel Winterburn who had moved to Arsenal.

I was a raw 20-year-old going from the Fourth Division to the top flight in London and having to replace a player who'd just won the club's Player-of-the-Year award in three successive seasons. Those first six months there were the hardest I've ever had in football.

They have a unique team spirit at Wimbledon. Newcomers get very special treatment. They don't accept you straight away. You have to earn their respect.

I didn't understand that when I first moved there. I didn't know what was going on. They never stop shouting at you. They'd say you were this and that because you'd come from the Fourth Division.

They were nicknamed the Crazy Gang and they certainly were. They did crazy things. You arrived at Wimbledon and you were thinking, 'that's not normal, you don't do that at normal clubs!'

The way the new boys were treated was one such example. You had to try and blend in and win them over. They were a very close group and had a bond between

One of the Wimbledon "Crazy Gang", Vinnny Jones

TOUGH GOING

For Manchester City's Terry Phelan

them and it wasn't easy for someone from the outside to break in. John Scales joined at the same time as me from Bristol Rovers and we both suffered. It was a hard time for us.

In some ways it was army style tactics and at one point I was ready to pack my bags and return to my home town, Manchester, because it was that bad. It was really getting me down.

However, I decided to stick it out. I thought, "I'm not having this. I am going to work hard, prove myself and gain their respect.'

I can remember it was March 1988 when I finally felt I'd done that, a full eight months after I'd joined! We played at Newcastle in a League match and for the first time in a Wimbledon shirt the lads said I'd done well and someone patted me on the back. I was one of them from then on.

The FA Cup run that season also helped. The lads wanted to win it so badly because of all the media criticism we received that we stuck together and the outsiders were accepted into the group.

I might not have enjoyed those early experiences at times but, looking back, it's a great and unique way and having come through that I was certain I could handle the pressure of being a £2.5 million player and that's the way it proved. I settled in at Manchester City no problem. The 'most expensive full-back label' never bothered me in the least.

Wimbledon Football Club itself also had an unusual way of treating its new buys. Normally top sides find their new players a house to live in or help out looking for places.

But not Wimbledon. My wife and I were just youngsters, sampling life in the bright lights for the first time. We had to walk around London and find a suitable flat. We had to sort out which were the better areas to stay in.

But that's how they operate. They let you get on with it. You have to learn somehow. It's no use the club being your mummy and daddy.

It was all experience, though. They say you should leave home when you are young and that's right. Both in football and off the field I have had a lot of experiences. I am only 25, but I feel like I'm 45 years old!

Having left Wimbledon behind me when I joined City I wasn't going to forget the 'apprenticeship' they gave me.

I wasn't going to relax because my career jigsaw had fitted together nicely and had achieved my ambition of playing for a Manchester club and was a £2.5 million player.

I learned a lot at Wimbledon and I'll not forget it. The Wimbledon spirit is still in me and always will be. Once that goes out of you, you've lost the battle. I want Wimbledon to think I have done them proud.

Moving to City has been the best thing that has ever happened to me. I have become a better player because of it. It's a big, homely club and I've loved every minute of it.

TELLY ADDICT!

Celtic's **Rudi Vata** was in a class of his own when it came to learning English!

IN 1979, back in Albania, I went along with 25,000 others to watch the local team, Partizan Tirana, take on a side from Scotland called Celtic in the European Cup.

Yet, here I am, 14 years on, as player at Parkhead!

Then again, I have grown up to realise that life is life, it can change every day and *nothing* should really surprise you.

It was a long route to Glasgow, and it started after I had established myself as an Albanian international.

The national team were due to play a match in Paris against France, and I had decided before the fixture that I was not going to return home, because of the situation with the communist regime there.

After the game, I met up with three Albanian supporters who lived in Nantes, and went down there to stay.

I had explained what I was going to do to officials who travelled with the Albanian party, and although they tried to persuade me not to, my mind was made up.

In Nantes, I obviously had nothing to call my own, but slowly I picked up the language — mainly through watching French television — and I also acquired an agent, who had seen me play.

Although I trained with Tours, a second division club, problems with my registration meant that was as far as it got. The real breakthrough came when communism broke down, and I was able to play for Albania again.

It was during a World Cup match against Ireland in Dublin — in which goals from John Aldridge and Paul McGrath meant we lost 2-0 — that Liam Brady spotted me.

When I was told about Celtic's interest, I wanted to try my luck in Scotland at once.

I played a couple of trial games on a pre-season tour, again in Ireland, and after that was delighted that I'd done enough to be signed.

Of course, this again meant a new culture AND language for me. But, after learning French, I was determined I would master English too.

I again spent a lot of time watching TV — programmes like Neighbours really helped, believe me! — and gradually picked it up.

But most important of all was adjusting to the football.

The game in Scotland is much faster and more physical than I was used to, so it meant I had to get myself into better condition.

After a few training sessions, which are definitely harder than I was used to, I felt much, much fitter.

However, I honestly believe that I have adapted better than most Albanians would to British-style football.

There are Albanians in France, Germany, at Dinamo Bucharest in Romania and many in Greece. But it would be very difficult for some of my compatriots to play here.

They are more used to playing with the ball. In Scotland, the game is all about running and hard and fast tackling.

Only younger Albanian players would be able to come over here and learn how to play this way.

It's far easier to adapt to the different ways the game is played when you are young and still learning.

Once a player back home has reached the age of about 25, I do not think he would be able to change his style to suit Scotland. But that is not a criticism, and I would like others to come over.

After all, there are many skilful players in the Premier League. Here at Celtic we have John Collins, Paul McStay and Tom Boyd as good examples. From the other clubs I liked Aberdeen's Eoin Jess as soon as I saw him.

Apart from being very good on the ball, they have the strength that continental players sometimes lack.

Then, of course, there is the support. The Scottish people are fanatical about football — there is just so much noise.

In Albania, there are big crowds, but they are not so noisy. They only really react when a goal is scored.

Indeed, everything, whether it be football or just my way of life, has changed so much in a short space of time. In fact, even writing for something like the Topical Times is a new experience!

When the communists were in charge back home, talking to journalists was not allowed!

But, despite all the differences, I do not forget that I am an Albanian. I enjoy nothing more than being able to play for my country.

And, although they are still living in Albania, I keep in regular contact with my parents and my brother Aleski, who is in Germany. We speak on the phone every two weeks and I send them some money when I can.

People in Albania don't have very much — but they are quite alike to Scottish people — very warm with good hearts.

I know just how lucky and happy I am to be playing for a club like Celtic.

GOING...!

GOING...

GONE...!

Wimbledon's John Fashanu and Robbie Mustoe, Middlesbrough, take a tumble as they chase a loose ball.

MIKE MARSH
Liverpool

MARK ROBINS
Norwich City

RAY PARLOUR
Arsenal
JVC

EOIN JESS
Aberdeen

LEAD BY

Newcastle United striker Gavin Peacock has more than just his team-mates and the fanatical Geordie fans on his side when he steps out on the St James' Park pitch.

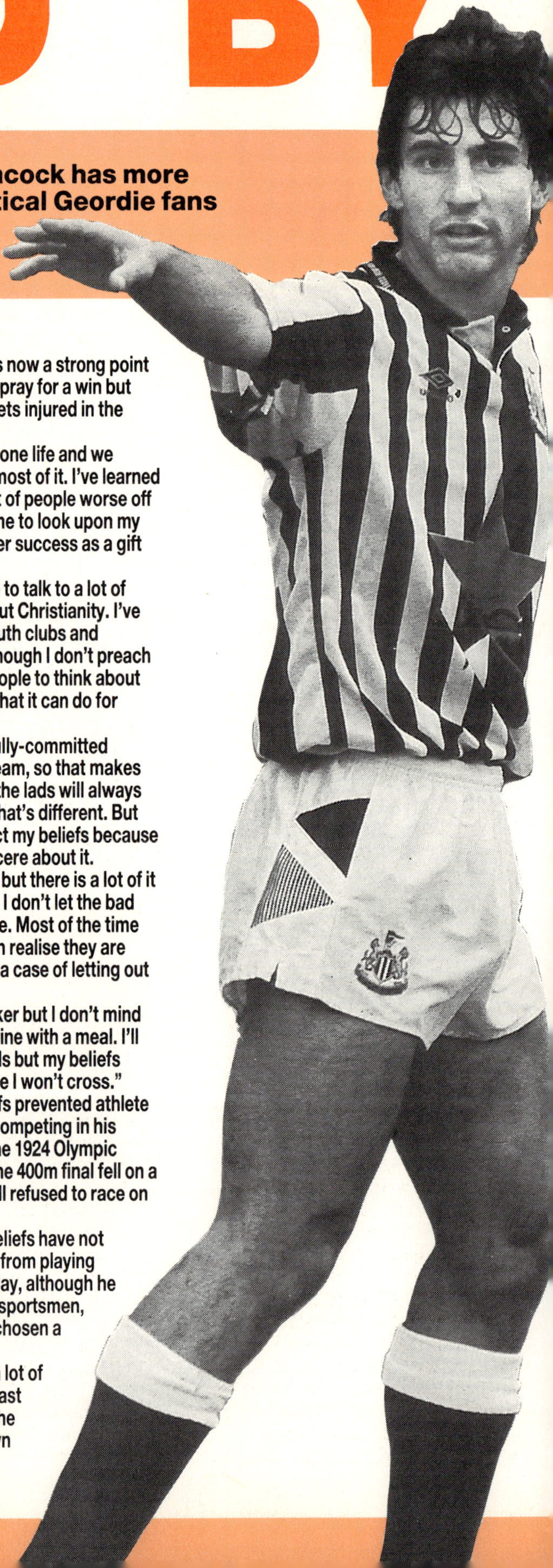

THE MAGPIES ace is a devout Christian and joins a growing list of footballers who have made a commitment to God. Others include Swindon Town player-manager Glenn Hoddle, Crystal Palace midfielder John Salako and Aston Villa striker Cyrille Regis.

Peacock has no problems mixing his faith with football. He shuns any opportunity to deliberately injure an opponent, but that doesn't stop him displaying a competitive spirit on the park.

Indeed, a glance at his achievements at United in the last couple of years, suggests that his beliefs may have helped the versatile marksman become a success at Newcastle.

He has been United's leading marksman over the last two seasons, taken over the captaincy and played a key role in the club's First Division promotion campaign last term.

"Religion is the central thing in my life," says Gavin. "I've always believed in God but it wasn't until I was 18 that I became a Christian.

"My mum, Lesley, started going to church and committed herself to God. I noticed a real change in her attitude afterwards. She became happier and much more at peace with herself.

"She used to smoke 40 cigarettes a day, but her faith enabled her to stop. She hasn't touched a cigarette since.

"I could see the effect Christianity was having on someone close to me and I was very impressed.

"At one time football meant everything to me. Although it's still important, it doesn't dominate my life any more. If I play badly and my team lose, it doesn't ruin my weekend.

"I now have a wife, Amanda, and we had a baby last May. I tend to be more relaxed on the pitch and I believe it helps my performances.

"I don't get ruffled and anxious any more. Discipline is now a strong point of my play. I don't pray for a win but just that no-one gets injured in the game.

"We only have one life and we should make the most of it. I've learned that there are a lot of people worse off than I am. I've come to look upon my material and career success as a gift from God.

"I've been able to talk to a lot of young people about Christianity. I've been invited to youth clubs and churches, and although I don't preach to them, I want people to think about Christianity and what it can do for them.

"I'm the only fully-committed Christian on the team, so that makes me different, and the lads will always pick on anything that's different. But the players respect my beliefs because they know I'm sincere about it.

"I don't swear, but there is a lot of it at St James' Park. I don't let the bad language upset me. Most of the time the lads don't even realise they are swearing. It's just a case of letting out their frustration.

"I'm not a drinker but I don't mind the odd glass of wine with a meal. I'll go out with the lads but my beliefs mean there is a line I won't cross."

Christian beliefs prevented athlete Eric Liddell from competing in his chosen event at the 1924 Olympic Games in Paris. The 400m final fell on a Sunday and Liddell refused to race on the Sabbath.

Those same beliefs have not stopped Peacock from playing football on a Sunday, although he understands why sportsmen, like Liddell, have chosen a different course.

"We did have a lot of Sunday matches last season because the games were shown live on television.

EXAMPLE!

That's the motto of Newcastle's Gavin Peacock

Eric Liddell — Never on a Sunday

"Some Christians wouldn't compete on a Sunday, but that's their decision. I consider it my job, therefore I've got to work on a Sunday.

"I might not be able to get to church until the evening if I'm playing on a Sunday. I remember one match at Barnsley, I found a local church in the morning and went in for prayers."

Gavin's career has taken off since the arrival of Kevin Keegan as manager at Newcastle in February 1992. He admits that his career took a while to get off the ground after his first brush with top flight football.

"I started my career at Queens Park Rangers, but made only 19 appearances in three years," he adds. "I was rather impatient and turned down the offer of a new three-year contract.

"I decided to drop down to Division Three with Gillingham because I wasn't getting regular first-team football. Later I moved up a division to Bournemouth and it was with them that I was spotted by Newcastle boss Jim Smith.

"That was a League match at St James' Park in February 1990. Funnily enough, I can remember speaking to a Bournemouth player before the game and saying that this would be a great club to play for. Six months later I was here.

"I feel I've matured since arriving at Newcastle. I'm now playing the best football of my career.

"I always considered myself an attacking midfield player, but Kevin Keegan has given me confidence to play up front and I'm really enjoying it."

He nearly left Newcastle at the start of last season when Middlesbrough were ready to offer £1.3m for him. But discussions with Keegan convinced him there was a golden future fcr the Magpies.

"I had talks with the boss and wanted to know what direction the club was moving in. I was in and out of his office so many times. In the end I decided to follow my instincts.

"Kevin convinced me there was no better place to play. He said a move away from Newcastle would be a disaster in the long term. I could have moved to a Premier League club, but I was convinced I'd have top-class football here. The only difference was I had to wait a few more months."

His decision to stay at St James' Park has not only led to the best spell of his career, it has also provided him with an unexpected new responsibility.

"The boss called me over one day during pre-season training and asked me if I wanted to be vice-captain," Gavin goes on. "I have to say I jumped at the chance.

"The previous captain, Brian Kilcline, was injured against Mansfield and I took over the reins.

"It's always difficult being heard when trying to organise things from an attacking position. In that respect, it would probably be easier for a midfield player to get his message across. However, I like to think I lead by example and others respond to the effort I put in.

"I believe the added responsibility has helped my game, and there's greater satisfaction in knowing I'm actually doing two jobs on the pitch."

IT'S QUIZ TIME!

RAY WILKINS

1. Who holds the record for the highest number of England caps?
2. Who were the beaten semi-finalists in last season's Coca-Cola Cup?
3. What team in Japan does Gary Lineker play for?
4. Fabio Capello is a coach for a top Italian club. Is it AC Milan, Juventus or Sampdoria?
5. Roy Wegerle was part of a two-man transfer between Coventry and Blackburn Rovers toward the end of last season. Who was the other player involved?
6. What were the scores between Rangers and Marseilles in the Champions League?
7. Which Scottish club plays at Somerset Park?
8. Whose Liverpool goal-scoring record did Ian Rush break?
9. Which manager recently retired after 21 years with the same club?
10. Who scored the winner in the 1992 European Cup Final at Wembley?
11. Name three clubs with the letter "X" in their name.
12. Q.P.R.'s Ray Wilkins has played for clubs in Scotland, Italy and France. Name them.
13. Who are the Valiants?
14. What was the score when England last played Scotland in a full international?
15. What nationality is Aston Villa's Mark Bosnich?
16. St Domingo FC was the first name of which English Premier League club.
17. Who plays at the Bernabeu Stadium?
18. What was significant about last season's FA Cup semi-finals?
19. If you were watching Grasshoppers play Young Boys which country would you be in?
20. In which city do Bristol Rovers play?

ANSWERS

1. Peter Shilton, 125 caps.
2. Blackburn Rovers, Crystal Palace.
3. Nagoya Grampus Eight.
4. AC Milan.
5. Kevin Gallacher, Coventry to Blackburn.
6. 2-2: 1-1.
7. Ayr United.
8. Roger Hunt's.
9. Jim McLean, Dundee United.
10. Ronald Koeman.
11. Halifax: Exeter: Oxford.
12. Rangers, AC Milan, Paris St Germain.
13. Charlton Athletic.
14. 2-0 England, 1989, Hampden.
15. Australian.
16. Everton.
17. Real Madrid.
18. They were both played at Wembley.
19. Switzerland.
20. Bath.

FABIO CAPELLO

NO HOLDS BARRED
as Chris Kiwomya, Ipswich Town, battles it out with Nottingham Forest's Scot Gemmill.

When the last batch of awards was being handed out at the tail end of last season, there was no provision for recognising the country's most improved player.

If there had been, it's unlikely you would have found a stronger candidate for the honour than Manchester United's midfield star, Paul Ince.

MIDFIELD

A rare Ince goal, v-Queens Park Rangers.

THE 26-year-old from Ilford, in his fourth season at Old Trafford, found his best form since joining the club from West Ham, earned a place in the England side from the first international outing of the season and emerged as the driving force behind United's bid for the Premier League Championship.

It was inevitable, too, that he would come to be known as the new Bryan Robson, having so effectively picked up the reins which had been dropped by the former England skipper during his long absence from the side.

It's a tag, however, which Ince is reluctant to accept, though he admits that he drew much of his inspiration from Robson on the road to finding his own peak form.

"When I arrived at Old Trafford, everybody said I was the new Bryan Robson, but that was unfair on me and unfair on Robbo," says Paul.

"I admit there are certain similarities in the way we play. For instance, I have always been able to tackle and that's one of Bryan's strengths. But we differ in many ways, too.

"Part of the problem was that I made my name by scoring two goals in a televised match for West Ham against Liverpool. It was great to score them, of course. But it gave people the wrong impression, because I've never been a goalscorer.

"Then, in my second match for United, I scored twice in a League Cup match at Portsmouth. The Press made a lot of it, and next day, I asked myself, 'What have I done?

"I knew that people would expect me to carry on scoring the way Robbo had always done. So I just put pressure on myself by scoring those goals, and in some ways I wished I had never done it. It just created expectations in the fans.

"I can win the ball and pass it, but I'm not another Bryan Robson in the box.

"Nevertheless, through playing alongside Bryan, I learned how to sense danger and what to do. I also learned how to gee up the other players.

"When I first played in the United side, I used to stand around on the pitch and wait for things to happen. Then Robbo would fly past me, run 30 yards and make a challenge. I'd watch it all and think, 'He's 33'!"

Robson's absence through injury, however, also helped to bring the best out of the player who, if not a carbon copy, has at least become a worthy successor at the heart of manager Alex Ferguson's team.

Ince goes on, "Growing older and wiser, and developing a sharper sense of responsibility helped me find my true form, and maintain a decent level of consistency. But it took a couple of years after my move from Upton Park.

"At the time of my transfer, in September 1989, I was not quite 22 and still had a bit of maturing to do.

"I'd also been used to playing in front of crowds of around 15,000 every week. Suddenly, I was running out to gates of 45,000. For a while, I was overawed, and that stopped me from producing my best football.

"It's hard to settle at a club like United. It takes you at least a year to understand what it's all about at Old Trafford.

"The fans really care about their football. It's so important to them. The club is so vast, you don't realise what it's like until you go there.

"Probably the biggest influence in shaping my maturity, however, was the birth of my son Thomas in January of last year.

"His arrival made me realise there was far more to life than just playing football. I became a family man and took all the responsibility that entailed. It also led to a far more sensible approach to everything I do.

"At one time, I regarded football as the be-all and end-all of life. It was an attitude which made things difficult for my wife, Claire. I was often unfair to her.

"For instance, if I'd had a bad game or had simply made a couple of bad errors, I'd let it prey on my mind for a long time afterwards.

"I'd go home after the match in a dreadful mood, take it out on Claire, and we'd usually end up having a row.

"The arrival of Thomas changed all that. Nowadays, if I've had an off-day on the pitch, I might still travel home in a bad mood. But as soon as I come into the house and see Thomas's face, it's all forgotten. I get on with enjoying my family life, and no longer worry about my bad games for too long."

MANCHESTER UNITED'S INCE-PIRATION!

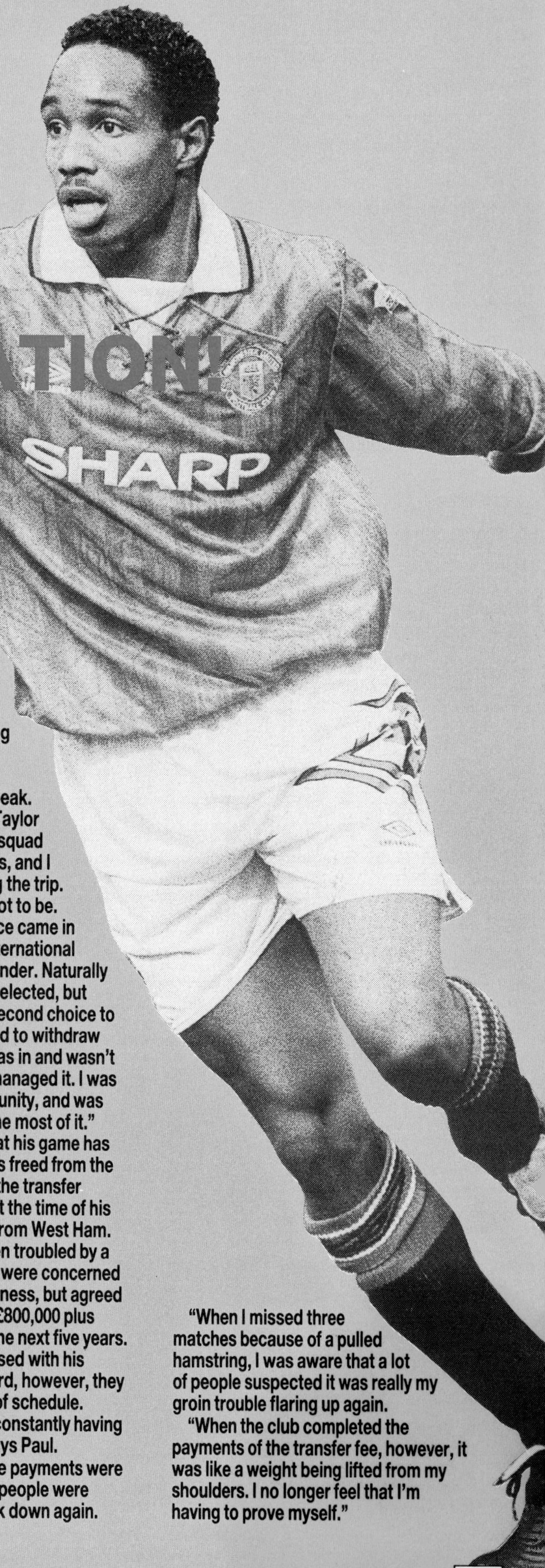

Ince also confirms that his change of attitude helped him to take the United midfield by the scruff of the neck and impose himself at a time when the side needed a leader. He goes on, "For the past year or so, a lot more responsibility was placed on my shoulders. Bryan Robson was missing for long spells and Neil Webb, prior to his move back to Nottingham Forest, was also missing from the side.

"All of a sudden I was the old head in midfield, playing alongside younger lads such as Darren Ferguson and Ryan Giggs. I was having to take on a lot more myself.

"With Robbo missing especially, I realised I had to carry the can and take the responsibility which he normally carries.

"The pleasing thing, however, was that though we needed somebody to be like him while he was out and I succeeded in doing that, I also carried on in the same vein when he returned."

Ince's progress was acknowledged last term when he became an England player, making his debut against Spain in the first international of the season, then going on to play a part in the World Cup qualifying campaign as England made their bid to secure a place in the Finals in the USA.

Having previously made just one appearance for the England B side against France, Ince was initially called up to the full squad as a stand-by player. His elevation took him by surprise.

He goes on, "When I played in the B side at Loftus Road, the season before last, I was used on the right wing, rather than my club role of central midfield.

"I believe if you really want to make an impression, you have to do it from your best position. I wasn't surprised at not being selected after that.

"However, I did think I had a chance of making the European Championships in Sweden in 1992. During the latter end of the season, my club form really started to hit a peak.

"Manager Graham Taylor did not have a settled squad leading up to the Finals, and I was hopeful of making the trip. Unfortunately it was not to be.

"However, my chance came in last term's opening international against Spain in Santander. Naturally I was delighted to be selected, but knew that I was only second choice to Trevor Steven, who had to withdraw through injury. But I was in and wasn't bothered at all how I managed it. I was grateful for the opportunity, and was determined to make the most of it."

Ince also reports that his game has improved since he was freed from the shackles imposed by the transfer arrangements made at the time of his move to Old Trafford from West Ham.

Because he had been troubled by a groin problem, United were concerned about his long-term fitness, but agreed to pay an initial fee of £800,000 plus £5,000 per match for the next five years.

United were so pleased with his progress at Old Trafford, however, they settled the fee ahead of schedule.

"At first, I felt I was constantly having to prove my fitness, says Paul.

"For as long as those payments were being made, I felt that people were waiting for me to break down again.

"When I missed three matches because of a pulled hamstring, I was aware that a lot of people suspected it was really my groin trouble flaring up again.

"When the club completed the payments of the transfer fee, however, it was like a weight being lifted from my shoulders. I no longer feel that I'm having to prove myself."

CULTURE SHOCK

DARREN ANDERTON looks set for a long international career — given a little time. The lanky winger, nicknamed 'Shaggy' after the TV cartoon character from Scooby Doo, is a self-confessed slow starter. Whenever he joins a new team, it always takes him a while to settle down. That was as true playing for Southampton under-15's team as it was at Tottenham Hotspur after his £1.7 million transfer from Portsmouth.

A SHY, quiet lad by nature, Darren needed to build up his confidence again after joining a big club like Tottenham. It would take him six months to score his first Premier League goal — ironically against his home-town team Southampton, where he had been a season-ticket holder as a kid.

But once he'd cleared that particular hurdle there was no stopping Darren. Suddenly he was everywhere, creating and scoring goals for both Spurs and the England Under-21 side. At last everybody realised why Terry Venables had splashed out so much money on a player who was only 20 when he arrived at White Hart Lane.

"I always said it would take me a while to settle into the routine of life at White Hart Lane," says Darren. "But once I had done that, the form came back very quickly.

"It was all a bit mind-blowing for a young lad like myself to come to a big London club. There were so many different things to get used to after my time with Portsmouth. At times during those first few months I thought I was never going to be the same player again. I couldn't ever see myself scoring for the team.

"Playing in the Premier League came as a bit of a culture shock to me. Suddenly I found myself up against quality full-backs every week, which was a rather different story to what I'd been used to playing for Portsmouth. I had to adapt to not having the space I'd enjoyed before.

"There was a lot expected of me when I first joined Tottenham. I was just sorry that I couldn't give the fans what they deserved during those early months. Thankfully, they stuck by me and were great when things started to go better for me later on.

"I'd expected to handle the whole situation much better. For several months I must have been just completely over-awed by the place and playing against the best players every week.

"I'd really been looking forward to taking on left-backs like Stuart Pearce every week, although that prospect did scare me a bit. But to start with I couldn't even get a place on the right wing. I had to settle for playing on the left and that didn't help at all.

"It was all very disheartening in the opening months of my first season. I couldn't seem to make it past the hour mark before I was being substituted. The lack of confidence was sapping my energy in games. I knew then that I would only be of use to the team when I'd shaken off the early nerves.

"Unfortunately, my chances of making a good impression were hampered when I developed a hernia problem. There was nothing for it but to have an operation. I'd actually first had the problem when I was still at Portsmouth. A long hard season at Fratton Park had caused the inevitable wear and tear on my body but the specialist thought rest would sort the problem out.

"It soon recurred when I started playing a lot of games for Tottenham. The physios quickly diagnosed the hernia and it was decided to get the operation done as quickly as possible.

"It was disappointing to have to go into hospital. On the other hand, I

The goal that put Portsmouth within minutes of Wembley. Liverpool's Mark Wright can't stop Darren firing Pompey ahead.

That's what the step up to the Premier League meant for Spurs' DARREN ANDERTON.

knew I wasn't 100% fit and the condition could only have deteriorated.

"So it wasn't the greatest of starts to my career at White Hart Lane. But things were to change quite quickly on my return.

"There's no doubt that I'd lost half a yard of pace with the problem. When I came back I felt sharper, my confidence returned and I was soon playing as well as I knew I could.

"I had a lot of people to thank for that — my friends, my family and all the Tottenham staff. They'd all had great faith in my ability to do well for the club.

"A most important factor was that I was settled at last. I'd moved into my own house and that made me feel much more relaxed. That change of mind soon started to show in my performances on the pitch."

What everybody wanted to see was the sort of form Darren had shown on Portsmouth's impressive FA Cup run. His dazzling displays had reached a fitting climax with his brilliant individual goal in the semi-final against Liverpool at Highbury.

That goal put Portsmouth within minutes of Wembley. They would later be denied in a dramatic penalty shoot-out, but Darren had shown he had a rare liking for the competition.

"There's something very special about the FA Cup," says Darren. "And I certainly felt a buzz at White Hart Lane when it came around last season. Tottenham is a club with a terrific FA Cup tradition. They almost expect to get to Wembley every year.

"The Cup also brought the best out in me as well. I don't know whether it was the memories of the previous year that inspired me, but I certainly enjoyed being back in the sudden-death environment of the cup-tie.

"My semi-final goal against Liverpool will always be one of the highlights of my career. The sporting reaction of Bruce Grobbelaar made it even better. He'd just been beaten in a vital game but he still had time to joke about it."

After that goal, Darren suddenly became hot property. Several big clubs were interested in securing his services. But they had to deal with his dad first.

Unlike many rising young stars, Darren didn't have an agent to do the talking for him — he relied on his football-supporting father to do that job.

Liverpool were still very interested in the young man they'd been tracking all season. One day a fan even asked Darren to sign a Liverpool shirt, so certain was everybody that he would be on the move to Anfield.

But Darren had other ideas. He fancied a move a little closer to home and that's when Tottenham entered the fray. Terry Venables quickly convinced him, and his dad, that he should go to North London.

Inevitably, Darren was soon being compared to Chris Waddle, a former favourite on the Tottenham wing. And as Waddle did in France, Darren likes the idea of testing himself abroad in the future.

But for now he is happy to continue making a big impact on the ground where his childhood footballing idol made his name.

"Glenn Hoddle was magnificent to watch. I thought he was a different class, a brilliant artist," says Darren.

They should be saying the same thing about Darren Anderton before too long.

CREDIT WHERE CREDIT'S DUE

That's what Sheffield United's DAVE BASSETT wants!

PREMIER LEAGUE football managers can be a dull bunch. Mostly morose, always non-commital, occasionally unapproachable, the men in charge could hardly double up as Public Relations officials.

Obviously, there are exceptions. And in the context of top-flight bosses, Sheffield United's Dave Bassett is just that.

He doesn't always do as the others do, nor necessarily say what they say, preferring instead to follow through his duties via his own often unorthodox, but usually successful, methods.

The 48-year-old Londoner, while enjoying hero status in certain parts of Sheffield, also has his detractors.

Often seen as the inventor of the long ball game, he has had to live with a large amount of criticism and huge lack of credit throughout his managerial career.

Despite his achievements at former club Wimbledon and more recently Sheffield United, most have yet to learn to appreciate anything to do with the game played by his sides.

A close look at Bassett's team will prove that the long ball can live in perfect harmony with more technical tactics. It's just a question of convincing those who remain unconvinced.

"Fans and the media don't come, watch us and then make an opinion," says Dave.

"They come with pre-conceived ideas that we only play the long ball game and that's all that they see. They see what they want to see. If it's convenient to ignore certain things then you will. I believe the Press and the media do that.

"There is very little I can do about that. But anyone who knows anything about them, anyone who has any intelligence or brains will look beyond that.

"A lot of people in this world are brainwashed. They believe what they read or what they hear someone say on TV. At the end of the day they don't make up their own minds.

"I suppose reputation goes before you and can make life difficult. People often don't appreciate what has been achieved at Wimbledon. They only see unsavoury things.

"But I suppose I've learnt to live with it now because it's a situation which has been around me for so long. A lot of people have jealousies, but I have sympathy for my players, because they sometimes don't get credit where it's due.

"But that's the way of life and life isn't very fair on occasions. We just have to put such things to one side and get on with playing the game.

"I didn't invent the long ball game, even though it would be easy to believe I did. Football has been around a long time, far longer than Dave Bassett has been a coach.

"I was playing the long ball game years ago and I could name numerous teams who used it to their advantage well before Wimbledon arrived on the scene.

"The 1970's Liverpool team played it that way when they used to knock it up to big John Toshack's head and onto Kevin Keegan! They certainly didn't pass it through the midfield.

"The Wimbledon side that reached the last eight of the FA Cup and finished in the top six of Division One a decade or so later didn't play long ball all the time. We played it at the right times, but also had skilful players such as Nigel Winterburn, Glyn Hodges, Kevin Gage and Dennis Wise who we used well.

"Unfortunately, people tend to forget things. They forget that Sheffield United developed and played differently as we moved up from the old Division Three to the Premier League.

"They also forget that we often played with a sweeper and moved the ball from the back in our first season at the top level.

"Nobody wants to see that, but when they see our goalkeeper dribble out of his box they immediately cry 'long ball.'

"But I see Manchester United's Peter Schmeichel, Leeds' John Lukic and David Seaman of Arsenal all do it. Few goalkeepers DON'T these days, but their sides aren't accused of being long-ball teams.

"Sheffield United may use that tactic more than others, but everybody must think it's a good idea because they've all grabbed it!

"I still get irritated by unfair criticism, but the people who give it have pre-conceived ideas. I don't know if they'll ever change, because for that to happen they have to want to change."

It's difficult to know just what Mr Bassett can do to install the first pieces of doubt in his critics' minds. Perhaps a season spent away from the relegation area would help.

"I thought we would do better than we did last season," Dave goes on. "At the start of the season I felt we could be a top-half team. I wanted us to be around there and able to creep up a bit if things went well.

"It was frustrating that didn't happen, because we showed what we could do by winning through to the semi-finals of the FA Cup and achieving good League results against the likes of Arsenal, Manchester United and Liverpool. We proved that on our day we can beat the best.

"Sheffield Wednesday had a very good season, reaching both cup finals, but I didn't really worry about that. It has been put to me that their success puts pressure on us here, but I don't look at it that way.

"They are a totally different club who can pay bigger wages and more expensive transfer fees than we can. Because of that they are able to attract a different type of player to those we can afford.

"I'm not envious of them, I'm just happy to get on with my job and do my best for Sheffield United. We are proud of what we are trying to achieve here, but it's great for the city if we both do well.

"I'm also proud of what I achieved at Wimbledon, but I don't look back to see which achievement was better. I only look back to those days to learn from what has gone before.

"I also learnt from my short time at Watford. I left Wimbledon to go there, but even though things didn't go well for me, there were aspects of the job at Vicarage Road I have used to help me since.

"I had a miserable time with the club and lasted much less than a year. It wasn't pleasurable by any stretch of the imagination. It's not something I would recommend or that I think is good for people.

"I don't necessarily think you only learn from your bad times or your mistakes. In my opinion you also learn from your successes.

"I knew before the end of that season I left Wimbledon that I would be leaving. My contract was up, I realised I wasn't going to be able to negotiate another and my relationship with the club was beginning to crack.

"After fourteen years it was a wrench to go and the whole thing affected me more than I thought it would. It got to me emotionally and, with hindsight, I would have dealt with things differently.

"The Watford move seemed ideal because of the chairman at the time, pop star Elton John. He attracted me to the move but, although I should have, I didn't realise how difficult adjusting and changing would be. I should have investigated the move more thoroughly.

"There were decisions I made there that again, with hindsight, I wouldn't have made now. But to be fair, I have made similar decisions here with Sheffield United."

The Watford saga has been largely forgotten, cast into the shadows by his successes elsewhere.

And if Bassett's top job suitabilities were questioned at that time, he has since answered them while helping The Blades regain their cutting edge. But what about the future and a really big job?

"I honestly don't think about them," he goes on. "I've got a fairly big job here, certainly a big club. We're not regarded as top eight, but we fall into the same category of a lot of other clubs just below that.

"But I'm a great believer in what will be will be. I don't go round thinking I'll be manager of such and such a club one day.

"People always said I'd never move from the south-east, that I was the Cockney lad who would never leave London. I dispelled that belief and now some say I'm not the type of person who would be wanted by the directors of a big club.

"I haven't got a clue if that's right or not and, to be quite honest, I don't care either. Directors judge managers as managers judge players. You make your decisions on what you feel you know."

DUE –

FITNESS FANATIC!

THIS year, Lou Macari added another honour to his already extensive collection.

His revitalised Stoke City team took the Second Division by storm, cruising to the Championship on the back of a 25-game unbeaten run.

Since taking over as Stoke manager in May 1991, Macari has led the resurgence of one of English football's sleeping giants.

City's revival has galvanised the whole town — crowds at the Victoria Ground regularly outdo many Premier League matches for attendance.

From the minute he arrived in the Potteries and took Stoke City by the scruff of the neck, Macari has set about making the team live up to their huge potential.

His uncompromising management style brooks nothing less than total commitment. Little wonder he has a reputation as a hard taskmaster.

He says, "I don't think I deserve that reputation. I have been called a disciplinarian because I ask players to do what I think I am paid to do — that is get them into a condition whereby they are fit enough to play 90 minutes of professional football.

"Footballers are no different to an artist going on at the London Palladium: they have to perform well in front of an audience.

"If my centre-forward goes out there with a big belly, it doesn't matter how much skill he has, he can't do the job if he can't get to the ball!

"The fans pay to see their team play for 90 minutes. If a player is ready to leave the pitch after 80, that's my responsibility.

"It's also my responsibility to try to extend their playing careers. I've never seen that work by encouraging them to drink regularly and keep late hours.

"When I went to Swindon, the backroom staff and I knocked the living daylights out of them in terms of fitness. But a lot of the older players who were there with me are still going.

"David Hockaday is still playing at 35. Chris Kamara is still playing at 35. Tim Parkin, also 35, is playing at Darlington and Steve White, who's 34, is still in the Swindon side.

"I played until I was 34 and I don't think for one minute I would have played until then if I'd been a boozer.

"Players always tell people they hate training and they hate running, etc. Personally, I think they say that because they don't want to make it look as if they're happy!

"You are daft if you don't believe this game is about moving your legs. If you didn't need legs I would still be playing — and I'm a better player than any we have here! I haven't lost my ability, I'm just older.

"I went to Old Trafford in 1972, which was Bobby Charlton's last season. I couldn't believe what he did. He was 35, yet he would run all over the pitch as if his life depended on it."

Macari admits he has made his fair share of mistakes, however. "At Swindon I expected the players to eat, drink and sleep football 24 hours a day. I quickly realised that will never happen," he says.

"New managers expect everyone to be as professional as Peter Shilton, who's still playing at 43. They're not.

"The game has changed so much since I was a player. If I was to expect the players here to perform and act in the manner of my old team-mates, I'd be wasting my time.

"At first it's hard to accept that not everyone is a Gordon McQueen or Bryan Robson. I would be tearing my hair out if I tried to make them all world-beaters.

"You have to be a certain type of character. I don't think managers who didn't want to win as players can do the job. That's a major ingredient.

"People criticise the win-at-any-cost attitude, but if you don't think like that, forget it — you're only playing at it.

"If you see this as just a job to pay the mortgage then you'll fail. You also have to enjoy it. I like winning and there's nothing else to it."

LOCAL HERO

Leeds United's DAVID BATTY

LEEDS UNITED suffered a year-long hangover after winning the League Championship two seasons ago.

Far from using that triumph as a springboard for further success, the Yorkshire club found themselves struggling to find the form which had captured the title.

Eliminated from the European Cup prior to the lucrative mini-league stage, they also struggled in the Premier League. Almost unthinkably, they flirted with relegation before completing the season languishing in the lower half of the table and didn't chalk up an away victory during the entire campaign.

If there was one bright spot for the Elland Road fans, however, it was the emergence of a new batch of youngsters to challenge the club's galaxy of high-priced stars for their first-team places.

Teenagers Robert Bowman, Jamie Forrester, Mark Tinkler, Kevin Sharp and Noel Whelan all enjoyed senior action during the latter half of last season, offering the prospect of better days ahead.

The rise of those kids has been a particular source of pleasure for midfield star David Batty, who is a champion of the club's youth policy and urges a continued emphasis on the search for and development of young talent.

Himself a product of Leeds' youth ranks, the 24-year-old England star made his United debut at the age of 18 and saw the club through their dark days in the old Second Division before achieving international honours and playing an instrumental part in winning the Championship.

In a bid to remain top dogs, manager Howard Wilkinson strengthened his squad with big-money stars and kicked off last season with a pool of players which had cost a total of £12.5 million. Only Batty and his midfield colleague Gary Speed, having come through the ranks, cost nothing.

Now Batty acknowledges that, had it not been for the failure to emulate the previous season's success, those kids would probably not have been given their chance. And he admits that, had Leeds not been in the Second Division at the time, he would probably have waited much longer for his own chance.

Says David, "Because of our Championship-winning success, and the fact that the club had spent a lot of money on strengthening the squad with proven stars, it looked for most of last season as though it would be extremely difficult for any young hopefuls to break through.

"Gary and I, who had come along a few years earlier, were very fortunate that the club's circumstances at the time allowed us the chance to establish ourselves in the senior side ourselves.

"When I made the step up, I was given a lot of publicity, probably because I was the local boy made good. Born in Leeds and having supported the club faithfully as a youngster, it made a good story. Gary and I had come up through the junior ranks together and grabbed our chance when it came along.

"But of course the club's status was far different then. Leeds were in the middle of an eight-year spell in the Second Division.

"We were lucky that we were ready for our chance at a time when things were not going well for the club. My own introduction to the first team came at a time when we were at the wrong end of the Second Division table.

"We were given time to secure our places and things only took off at Elland Road after we had established ourselves as regulars.

"Circumstances are vastly different now to how they were then. If we had been knocking on the door of the first team during the past couple of seasons and when the club were winning the League Championship and spending millions on big-name stars — I'm pretty certain it would have taken a lot longer to make the breakthrough.

"Nevertheless, I'm a believer in the principle that, in football, anybody with the ability to perform at the top will reach that level sooner or later. So I'm sure I would have been given my chance eventually, even if I'd had to wait a bit longer.

"However, having emerged with Leeds and, like Gary, gone on to play at international level, it does prove the value of the big clubs maintaining a well-run youth system.

"In order to compete with the best, a big club like Leeds will obviously be in the market whenever top-class players become available, and pay big prices to sign them.

"But we can't allow that fact to obscure the need to bring our own young players through the ranks. Having your own production line gives you a solid base.

"There are youngsters at Elland Road now with tremendous potential, yet probably find the route to the top more difficult to negotiate than I did since they are competing with more big-name players.

"When things are going well and the big stars are holding down their places, I can appreciate the frustration which the younger players must feel. They must wonder at times what it will take to make the breakthrough.

One of Leeds' rising stars — KEVIN SHARP

"In recent years it has been hard enough for some of us who have been regulars in the first team to be certain of our places.

"During the season we won the Championship, I believed we had one of the strongest midfield combinations in the country, yet we couldn't take our places for granted because the competition within the club was so intense.

"Then, last term, there were many occasions when I looked across at the substitutes' bench and saw players such as David Rocastle and Steve Hodge sitting there waiting for a chance to get on.

"When you know there are such quality players ready to take your place at the first opportunity, you don't need any other incentive to step up your game.

"And though you are never conscious during the game of whether you are playing well enough to stay on, as soon as one of the substitutes starts to strip for action, you automatically wonder if it's going to be you who will be replaced."

The opportunities given to those youngsters by manager Howard Wilkinson lately means the competition is now even hotter. But Batty says, "It can only keep everyone on their toes."

THE MIGHTY QUINN!
Coventry's Mick Quinn gets in a shot despite the attention of John Scales, Wimbledon.

CUP-TIE CRAZY!

THAT'S MILLWALL'S KASEY KELLER

Millwall goalkeeper Kasey Keller loves playing in the Coca-Cola Cup, and particularly the F.A. Cup. The American star loves the special atmosphere of cup ties — because there is no sporting equivalent in the USA. No professional sport in America offers the chance for a 'David' to take on a 'Goliath'.

No minor league team gets the opportunity to take on the major leaguers in any sport.

BUT next summer, Keller will get the chance to stage his own giant-killing performance on home territory.

The Millwall star will be fighting for a place at the centre of World Cup '94. America hosts sport's biggest event, a tournament in which he will be one of the underdogs battling to upset the odds against the best in the world.

"I first started getting really interested in soccer during the 1982 World Cup Finals," reveals Keller. "At the time of the 86 finals, I decided soccer was going to be my sport. By 1990, I was in the US squad for the finals in Italy, although I didn't play. Now I hope my experience with Millwall will earn me a place in the side for '94.

"People will see the US as the no-hopers of the tournament, as they did in Italy. But we are learning all the time, and the US team could surprise a lot of people.

"Last year we won the US Cup 92, organised by the United States Soccer Federation. We beat the Republic of Ireland and Portugal, and drew 1-1 with Italy.

"The problem for the American players has been the lack of top class experience at home. There is no major league soccer. That's why I came to England to play.

"It doesn't matter how hard you train and practise at home. You can only really learn and improve from playing in top competition.

"Things like reading the game are so important. That can only come from experience.

"Playing for Millwall is a total learning experience for me. It's great to play in cup competitions to get the feeling of playing teams from different levels of the game.

"There is nothing comparable to the FA Cup in American sport. There's no mixing of leagues. A little league team never gets the chance to play the superstars.

"To play in the FA Cup was always like a dream for me. I watched a lot of finals on TV at home in Seattle. The Coca-Cola Cup is not so well known, but you can still meet teams from different leagues.

"At Millwall last season I played against Leyton Orient from Division Two, when we were expected to win, and then against Arsenal when we were expected to lose.

"I saw both sides of the coin, and both ties were very close. It's all great experience for me to take back to America for the World Cup."

Keller will be fighting for the goalkeeping slot with the established Tony Meola. He also tried his hand in England, but failed to earn a contract.

TURN OVER FOR A SUPER WORLD CUP FEATURE!

BORA MILUTINOVIC

SIMPLY

Both Kasey Keller and Tony Meola will be at the heart of an American bid to stage the best World Cup ever. It is asking a lot for the Americans to outdo the Italians, but preparations are already nearing completion.

SILVERDOME, DETROIT. Capacity 73,000 — Home of the Detroit Lions and venue for the first-ever indoor World Cup tie.

NINETEEN different cities applied for the right to stage matches, and nine were eventually selected. They form three regional groups of three centres.

Los Angeles, San Francisco and Detroit will stage first round matches in World Cup groups A and B. Chicago, Boston and Dallas will host groups C and D. New York, Washington and Orlando will handle games from groups E and F. The opening match, involving the holders, Germany, will take place at Soldier Field, Chicago, on Friday June 17, home of the Chicago Bears.

The final, on July 17, will be played in the Rose Bowl, Los Angeles, which can hold 102,000 fans.

For the first time in World Cup history, matches will be played indoors — at the fabulous Pontiac Silverdome Stadium in Detroit. The first game will feature the USA. The silverdome holds 73,000 spectators, The roof is made of a teflon canopy, held aloft by atmospheric pressure. The Americans are determined to get everything right at the Silverdome — particularly the pitch. Normally it is Astro-turf, but the World Cup will be played on natural grass.

As soon as FIFA authorised the use of the stadium, the Yanks began experiments on growing grass indoors. They built a special small-scale replica of the silverdome to simulate conditions, and test different grasses.

Scientists at the University of Michigan tested the growing properties of different seeds. They settled on a mixture of Kentucky blue-grass. The turf was initially grown in California in hexagonal metal frames, and then transplanted to the Silverdome. It was tried out at the US Cup 93 this summer, when England met Germany. The turf was then taken up and preserved. It will be re-laid for the World Cup. The Giants Stadium in New York will also have turf laid over the artificial pitch.

For the first time, the World Cup organisers have to cope with the problem of different time zones. Los Angeles, for example, is three hours behind New York. There are four different time zones across America, and matches are to be played in three of them. Kick-off times have to be adjusted to make sure that matches kick-off simultaneously. Matches will start at 12.30, 16.00 or 19.30 New York time — which means 5.30 pm., 9.00 pm. or 12.30 am in Britain.

Because there is no proper soccer league in the US, many of their top international players are under

THE BEST!

The Chicago Bears' SOLDIER FIELD. 1990 winners Germany will kick-off proceedings on June 17th.

ROSE BOWL, Los Angeles. The venue for the World Cup Final.

contract to the USSF. It's like Alan Shearer and Paul Gascoigne being employed by the Football Association, instead of by Blackburn and Lazio.

But it does mean that USA team manager Bora Milutinovic can get his squad together for long periods as and when he wants. Every single international team manager involved in the qualifying scramble would envy his access to players.

Milutinovic is confident of making a success of his preparations for the finals.

"The American public is larger, and more interested in soccer than you think," he says.

"The American people have a 'can do' attitude, and a character which produces miracles. That's why I think we can surprise everybody, and become the Denmark of the 1994 World Cup."

No matter how the US team fares, however, the Americans are determined to make it a memorable World Cup. They plan to use the event as the platform on which to build a professional league in future.

Their original document, prepared for FIFA at the time of their bid to stage the finals, in 1988, was clear. America's mission was 'To present history's best World Cup, and to build a legacy for soccer in the United States.'

In conjunction with the tournament, the Yanks plan hundreds of coaching clinics throughout the country. They will spend huge sums on re-furbishing soccer grounds, or building new ones for local communities.

To help television viewers identify the stars on view in the finals, every player will wear his number, on the back and front, and have his name on the back of his shirt.

For the past two years, the Americans have been running what they call an Educational/Awareness Program to popularise the game.

"The problem for soccer in America is that the 'big three' pro sports, baseball, basketball and grid-iron football, take up all the time on television," admits Millwall goalkeeper Kasey Keller.

"Ice-hockey is also getting very big, and claiming peak time viewing. If there is any soccer, it gets stuck on at 2 am. in the morning.

"However, I'm sure soccer would get very popular if it was shown at a decent time — and it will get a lot of exposure during the World Cup."

The countdown is underway. Stand by for lift-off of World Cup 94 in June — US style.

WORLD CUP WORLD-

NEVILLE SOUTHALL, EVERTON

NEVILLE SOUTHALL has rightly been regarded by pundits in this country as one of the best goalkeepers in the world.

He's consistently performed heroics for Everton and Wales for over a decade at the highest levels of the game.

But if Nev isn't viewed overseas as one of the best in the world, then it's because he's never had a chance to prove himself on the biggest stage of all.

For while the World Cup Finals are a showpiece for the game's finest footballing talent, some world-class players remain destined never to appear.

With Wales' bid to reach the World Cup Finals in the United States next year once again floundering, it looks certain that for some players their last chance of performing in the finals has also gone.

It's nothing new for the cream of Welsh football during recent decades. The Principality hasn't qualified for the World Cup Finals since 1958.

Southall and Welsh team-mates Mark Hughes, Dean Saunders and Ian Rush deserve a crack at the World Cup finals, but also look likely to miss out.

Such disappointment would be especially cruel to Southall. The 34-year-old Everton and Wales 'keeper has been the most consistent performer in Britain for over a decade now, winning League Championship, FA Cup and European Cup Winners' Cup medals with the Goodison Park side.

Nev tells me, "It's sad Wales haven't been to the World Cup Finals for so long, especially when you consider all the world-class players we've produced.

"I like to think that while Wales have missed not competing, the World Cup Finals have missed having a Welsh team represented.

"It's a vicious circle. We have never done enough to get a good seeding for major competitions. As a result, we've always faced tough competition.

"We always seem to be in the most difficult group. I'm sure if we had been seeded a couple of times we would have reached the Finals.

"Unfortunately, it's not the best twenty-four nations which qualify. I don't think anyone would doubt we're better than Zaire, or such like. The rise of football in the Third World means there is a reduction in qualifying places for European sides. That will hit countries like Wales badly.

QUEST FOR CLASS KEEPER!

"You've got to trust yourself to fate. Sometimes it works in your favour, sometimes not. I've had loads of success with Everton, so maybe my Wales career is the flip side.

"The law of averages suggests our luck will change at sometime. I hope I'll still be around when it does."

Neville is on course to become the most capped player for his country. He's fast catching up with Peter Nicholas's Welsh record of 73 caps.

"I never look at the number of caps I've got," he goes on. "I think records are for looking back on when your career is over.

"Of course, if I do beat Peter's record I'll be very proud. But my main concern will be to get into the squad for the next game."

While Southall admits he's not getting any younger, he refuses to accept this is his last chance to make a World Cup Finals.

"You can't afford to think like that," he adds. "The way I look at it is, if we don't qualify for the USA, all I can do is wait for the start of the next campaign.

"Of course, it may turn out to be my last chance. Who knows what will happen? I could get injured or be dropped.

"I've learned never to take anything for granted. I was on course to make my 400th League match for Everton last season and then I was sent off. It was the second time I had been sent-off that season. Previously, I'd been dismissed just ONCE in my whole career.

"At present time, my form is holding up, but a footballer is always faced with the risk that he can lose form very quickly. However, don't expect me to announce my retirement for a while.

"I think I can keep going for several more years yet. I've just got to look after myself. You only have one body, so you've got to make the most of it.

"It's a case of working on my fitness. I have to do what's necessary. I enjoy training, but I won't do it to the point where it becomes a grind."

Observers noted that Southall was on the Highfield Road pitch at 10.30 a.m. practising for a League match against Coventry City last season. Admittedly, it was a 12.30 kick-off, but it does show the amount of preparation Southall puts in.

"I usually go out a couple of hours before kick-off," he continues.

"I go through my stretching routine, kick a few balls about and find my bearings on the pitch. If goalkeepers haven't properly warmed up, it does tend to show in matches.

Another world-class Welshman — Manchester United's Ryan Giggs.

"When it's an away match I'm especially keen to get to the ground early and out on the pitch. I don't like hanging about in hotels. I much prefer fresh air."

However, even Nev draws the line somewhere. He saw the funny side in reports that he had his breakfast on the pitch at Coventry.

"I might have had a bite at something, but it certainly wasn't my breakfast!"

A ROVER'S RETURN

Blackburn to Aberdeen transfer meant a home-coming for

DUNCAN SHEARER

Looking back, the seeds of my move to Aberdeen were sown one summer's day in June 1990 when the Football League 'relegated' my former club Swindon from the old First Division, without ever playing a game, because of 'financial irregularities.'

It was a decision I did not agree with and never will, but I can't deny it altered my career, and everyone else's at the club.

As soon as the League had delivered their verdict, Swindon were in trouble. We had a good team then, and because of the anticipation of First Division football for the first time, the players had been awarded healthy contracts.

Of course, we ended up in the Second Division, and the club really struggled for money after that.

By the end of 1991-92, it was obvious that they would accept the first big offer they received for any of the staff before the transfer deadline.

As it transpired, I was that player! Aberdeen were interested, I'd agreed terms with Notts County, but it was to Blackburn that I eventually went.

The club was, and still is, unique. The money available to Kenny Dalglish was far above what any other club had, and I make no bones about saying I went there more or less for financial security.

WILLIE MILLER

The set-up at that time was geared entirely to getting Blackburn into the top flight, and I think, deep down, I realised if that was achieved, because of the incredible resources, there would be more expensive arrivals than myself.

So it proved. Maybe I would have had a chance in the Premier League with Alan Shearer's ligament injury keeping him out for so long, but I suspect most of my time would have been spent in the reserves.

I wouldn't have sulked. I'd have been big enough to take that, but I know I would have been hoping that someone moved for me before I went too stale.

To my surprise, Aberdeen came in for me again. I saw no reason why one of the top Scottish clubs shouldn't want me — after all, Blackburn had — but after missing out once, I was delighted Willie Miller came back.

To be honest, they probably couldn't have competed with Blackburn the first time round, but circumstances had changed. To Kenny Dalglish's credit, he said he wouldn't stand in my way, so I was on my travels again.

I couldn't have picked a better place to return to Scotland. It's not that far from Fort William, where I was brought up, and my present wife Michelle had worked there before I met her.

Indeed we'd spoken about living in the Granite City once my playing days in England were over, so the transfer was perfect in that respect.

So it just left me to concentrate on what I was doing on the field. And, above all, I was determined to make a good start.

That stemmed from my Swindon days. I got off on the wrong foot there, and it wasn't something I wanted to repeat.

I'd arrived as the club's most expensive signing, scored a lot of goals pre-season, then when the real thing started, fired blanks for 10 games! I wasn't the most popular man and it did get to me.

And no matter what anyone says, I still maintain turning the Swindon fans' opinions of me around is my greatest achievement in football.

After an awful beginning, I went on to score 16 goals that season. The next season I managed 25 and was voted their 'Player of the Year.'

But it's difficult. Once a man has made his mind up about you, he's stubborn and unlikely to change it no matter how well you do.

They pay their money and, in my opinion, are entitled to criticise you. It's up to you to prove them wrong.

At Pittodrie, I needn't have worried. In my first Premier Division match, against Hibs, we won 3-0 and I scored two. The fans seemed to take to me immediately.

But it's not just me. Willie Miller now has four strikers at his disposal, and I think we are all delighted by each other's presence.

From my point of view, and Mixu Paatelainen's, it's great to have Eoin Jess and Scott Booth available to do the running outside the box. I believe the young lads appreciate that we take the weight off them.

It wasn't just up front, though, that the team was gelling. After a poor season by Aberdeen's standards, results had improved again — although I must admit even I was slightly surprised by the extent they had.

After playing Highland League clubs in our pre-season preparations, it was wrong of me to judge the team, but that's what I'd done.

There were hiccups on the way though. Getting sent-off against Rangers at Ibrox in a League match was a disappointment, maybe not so much for me, but for a lot of my relatives who were all there.

Our Skol Cup final defeat, 2-1 to Rangers, was also a sore one. It was only afterwards that I realised how close we had come — I still believe we could have nicked it on penalties — but it stood us in good stead and proved we had no reason to fear Walter Smith's men.

I also managed to pick up a medial ligament injury, through a block tackle, but that was hardly surprising. Although the game down south is faster, it's much more physical and there's far less time on the ball in Scotland.

On the whole, however, I would say coming north has worked out perfectly for me. I've even been mentioned in Scotland terms, which was a real shock as I genuinely thought the boat had passed me by and there's been no REAL improvement in my play since I came up from England.

But that's what comes of being at one of the top clubs and getting so much coverage. It was a great honour.

Now my aim has to be to win medals, something I've not yet managed to do. I played most of my career in England in the old Division Two, where there was less chance of success in the cups. That's not the case at Aberdeen.

Even if I can't win medals though, I've been told I'm the first prolific marksman at the club since Frank McDougall, so it's nice to make my mark there. But I do believe I will have success.

So far my biggest day was Swindon's Wembley play-off win over Sunderland, which all went wrong. Yet as I said, it paved a round-about way to Aberdeen!

Another bargain buy from Blackburn —
LEE RICHARDSON

ALAN MAIN
Dundee United

JOHN WARK
Ipswich Town

MARADONA
Seville

GIANLUCA VIALLI
Juventus

"PLAY ME A

That's Eddie McGoldrick's Plea To Jack Charlton

LAST season wasn't a good one for us at Crystal Palace. In fact, we had a terrible time.

We'd been full of optimism as ever at the start of the first ever Premier League season. But we never really got going and it turned out to be one long traumatic struggle against relegation.

We were dogged by injuries and suspensions and didn't have a regular strike-force all season. Nobody could blame the likes of Ian Wright and Mark Bright for leaving the club. They'd probably outgrown Palace by the time they left.

Looking back I know I learned a lot about myself as a player during the course of that difficult 1992-93 campaign. I'm sure the whole experience has made me a better player.

It was really a story of a season of two distinct parts for me. For the first few months I was playing in my usual attacking midfield role and scoring more goals than ever before for Palace.

There was a lot of talk in the newspapers about the bonuses I was on for scoring goals. But that wasn't important to me, I just wanted the team to do well.

With Mark Bright leaving for Sheffield Wednesday early in the season, we needed as many goals from other players as we could muster. So I was pleased with my return for the first part of the season and I really fancied myself to go on and score a lot more. I think I would have ended up with sixteen or seventeen goals.

But former manager Steve Coppell had other plans for me. He decided it was time to use me as a sweeper.

That was fine by me. I'd been asking the boss to play me there for a long time. I'd played much of my early football there for Nuneaton and Northampton and I honestly felt Palace would get the best out of me there. When I first joined the club, I was only young and the boss thought I was still learning the game. The priority then was getting promoted from the old Division Two and he couldn't take the risk on me as a sweeper.

Last season he finally changed his mind. So it was goodbye to goal-scoring and time to concentrate on stopping them at the other end. With the way things were going for us at the time, we certainly needed to tighten up at the back.

Our only bit of success last season came in the Coca-Cola Cup. We played some great football to get through to the semi-finals before it all came to a halt against Arsenal.

Ironically, we'd gone all through the competition without our top scorer Chris Armstrong. He was unfortunately cup-tied before he joined us as Mark Bright's replacement. We really missed him badly against Arsenal but he more than made up for it with some vital League goals.

There was a lot of pressure on Chris following the likes of Mark Bright and Ian Wright. But he quickly proved himself to be a top-class replacement.

When a new player comes to Palace, I've always seen it as my responsibility to make him feel as welcome as possible. It's in my nature to be friendly.

A new player can have all sorts of problems when trying to settle into a new club. If he doesn't feel happy at the place, he's unlikely to be much use on the pitch.

That's what happened with Welsh international Paul Bodin when he came to Palace a couple of years ago. He found it difficult to adjust to our style of play and before long he was on his way back to Swindon.

That was a shame because he was a quality player and we never seemed to have a regular left-back after he left the club. I tried very hard to make Paul feel welcome but he never managed to settle. The same thing happens to a lot of players throughout the League.

NYWHERE!"

Last season I realised I was one of the senior players at the club. That brought extra responsibilities with it. I had to take some of that extra burden off the young players' shoulders.

Switching to the defence inevitably meant I got booked more often then before. Tackling has never been a problem for me but the more challenges you make, the more likely you are to pick up a yellow card.

I started to feel guilty every time I was cautioned as the season progressed. With the threat of suspension looming for myself and other senior players, we knew we could be left short at just the wrong time.

Despite enjoying the move to the sweeper position last season, I almost missed playing in the midfield. And I'm not sure what the positional move did for my international prospects with the Republic of Ireland team. If I'd kept playing in midfield and scoring goals, Jack Charlton might have given me a few more starts.

My international future is probably in an attacking midfield role. But at least being able to play in different positions does make me a versatile man for the manager to have in his squad. In any case, I still think I've got time on my side at international level.

When I was 25 I thought all that had passed me by. I was just happy to be playing at a good level with my club and I never imagined myself turning out in the green shirt of Ireland.

Now my attitude has changed, I'm still only 28 and as long as Jack Charlton keeps picking me I've got a chance in being involved in all the big games.

Being part of the Irish squad is a unique experience. It's just a constant reminder of how far I've come since my non-League days.

Getting into the Irish team is very difficult. We have one of the best midfields in Europe with players like Andy Townsend, Ray Houghton, Steve Staunton and Roy Keane. It's very difficult for me to get in past one of those four.

It's no easier to find a place in the back four. I'm just going to have to be patient.

It will be worth waiting for because I think some very exciting things are going to happen with Eire in the next year or two. Big Jack Charlton will make sure of that.

STOOP TO CONQUER!

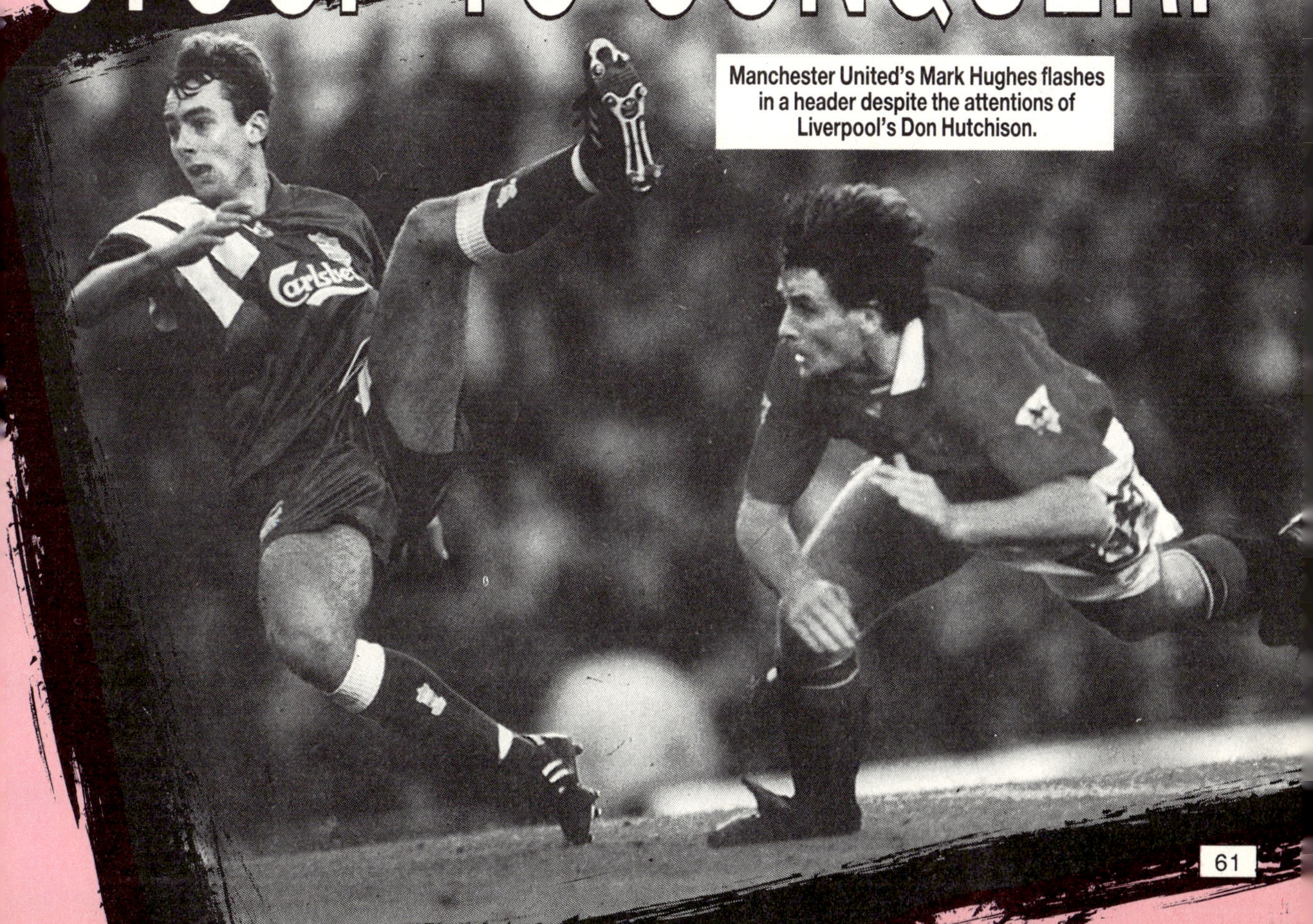

Manchester United's Mark Hughes flashes in a header despite the attentions of Liverpool's Don Hutchison.

COVER TACKLER

One of Ian Kennedy's pastimes is football. But he doesn't play it or watch it — he DRAWS it! Dundee-born Ian is a regular contributor to the front covers of the Football Picture Story Monthly, and his style is easily recognised by devotees of the publication.

"I joined D. C. Thomson's, the publishers, straight from school and became a staff artist working in the studio. I was asked to draw almost anything and that was a great grounding for when I went on to become freelance."

Ian's versatility was put to good use, drawing war stories, girls' adventure, boys' adventure, pony stories and then — more recently — football.

Ian played football at school and with the Boys Brigade but nowadays his contact with the sport is only by drawing covers and watching the occasional TV game.

"When it comes to football, I'm something of a traditionalist. I was brought up in the day of the 2-3-5 formation where wingers were IN and defensive tactics were OUT. Although some teams are playing what I call football, I still hark back to the days of outside rights, centre forwards and left-halfs." (That's wingers, strikers and midfielders!)

"Alan Gilzean was one of my favourites, as was Johnny Haynes."

Although he enjoys drawing football, Ian's number one love is aeroplanes, where his artwork is much sought after by RAF open days and displays. Versatility, indeed! Now, is there a story somewhere about a football-playing jet pilot . . . ?!

CHRIS ARMSTRONG
Crystal Palace

BRIAN GAYLE
Sheffield United

PAT NEVIN
Tranmere Rovers

MAN OF DESTINY

TONY ADAMS (Arsenal)

COULD 1994 be the year that Arsenal captain Tony Adams finally fulfils the destiny predicted for him by the late England skipper Bobby Moore?

Tragically, Moore died earlier this year without seeing Adams develop into the commanding world class defender the 1966 World Cup star believed he would become.

Moore forecast years ago that Adams would follow his own footsteps and become an inspirational captain for England.

By leading Arsenal to two major cup finals last season, and starring for England in the World Cup qualifying campaign, Adams is starting to live up to Moore's hopes for him.

The Arsenal star has certainly stepped up a level in the last year.

"All I've wanted in the last year or two is to get some respect from the media for my ability," says Tony.

"Last season went really well, and all of a sudden people began saying nice things about me.

"It's very flattering that Bobby Moore should have compared me to him, but I

Tony with the first of his Wembley double — the Coca-Cola Cup.

would never try to make that comparison. I can only play my own game.

"I can't even think about the England captaincy. That's nothing to do with me. I'm just happy to have been back in the England squad in the last year.

"At the start of last season I did hope for a chance. If it came, I knew I had to take it.

"Fortunately I got that opportunity. I thought it might be the only one I would ever get, and I had to make the most of it.

"In the past few years I've had a lot of setbacks. Things have not been easy for me, on or off the field.

"It was very disappointing to miss out on the World Cup finals in 1990. Mark Wright was preferred to me at the last minute.

"Then last year I was put on stand-by for the European finals in Sweden, when Mark was injured. But UEFA refused to let me take his place.

"But those are the kind of things you have to accept, and put behind you. You have to be able to forget the disappointment, and get on with the game.

"At least the call-up for Sweden showed I was close to the squad. I felt if I played well for Arsenal I would have a chance of getting back in.

"Now I need to work hard to stay there."

Adams has been Arsenal captain for more than five years, having taken over from England left-back Kenny Sansom in time to lead the Gunners out at Wembley for the 1988 Littlewoods Cup final.

That ended in defeat by Luton, and last season was his first chance to pick up a trophy at Wembley. Adams led Arsenal to success in both Coca Cola and F.A. Cup Finals. However, in between he twice collected the Football League Championship at Highbury.

Adams has always been a natural leader.

"I have always been a natural 'organiser'," admits Tony. "At school I was always picking teams, and sorting out who should play where.

"I like winning. It doesn't matter who my team-mates are, I'll have a go at them if I don't think they are fulfilling their potential.

"In only my third England game, against Brazil, I had a right go at our right-back Gary Stevens.

"He went forward and left us with a two-on-two situation. I gave him a right volley.

"I apologised to him afterwards, but he said 'fair enough, it got me going'. I'll always be talking a lot on the pitch, no matter who is captain."

Few people remember Adams' international debut — thanks to Gary Lineker. He began his England career in Spain on the night that Lineker slammed four goals past his Barcelona team-mate Andoni Zubizarreta.

"Gary Lineker claimed all the limelight, and in a way that was good for me," admits Tony.

"Ask anybody about what happened in that match, and they'll say 'Gary Lineker scored four goals'. Nobody will ever say 'Tony Adams made his debut'.

"There was no real pressure on me, because Gary had stuffed the Spaniards before they got going. But it was still great experience.

"It was a fantastic feeling to play my first match for England. I will never forget it.

"Every player is given two shirts for each international match — one to keep and one to swap with opponents.

"I kept both from my debut game. I couldn't bear to part with my first England shirt."

Despite that winning start, Adams' England career has been a stop-and-start affair. He's had to overcome a lot of 'stick' from the media.

But leading Arsenal to the League Championship in 1989, at the age of just 22, demonstrated his strength of character. It showed through very early in his football career.

Adams won his first football medal at the tender age of six and a half — in competition with boys three years older.

"My dad ran a boys' team called Dagenham United, and even went on the F.A. Coaching course to get his badge, so that he did things right," recalls Tony.

"I owe a lot to him. He was a keen amateur player, and taught me everything as a kid.

"The team I played for stayed together for about seven years. One season we won every match, and scored 161 goals losing only 1 — and that was an own goal!

"At the start I was playing against much older, stronger boys, and I learned how to cope. That stood me in good stead when I first played for Arsenal at the age of 17."

Tony Adams is now 27. It seems amazing that he has been playing league football for ten years, and is only now reaching his peak.

The Arsenal skipper hails from the same East London area as Bobby Moore. He was born ten weeks after the former West Ham captain lifted the World Cup, in 1966.

It could now be the right moment for him to start to dominate the scene the way Moore predicted.

WHAT GOES UP . . .

Tony Adams' celebrations after the Coca-Cola Cup Final turned sour when match-winner Steve Morrow was injured just after the final whistle . . .

YEE-SS! I've just scored my first goal for the Gunners, and it's a winner at Wembley!

Tony Adams' 'over-the-shoulder' to Ray Parlour goes wrong . . .

. . . and Steve hits the deck! OUCH!

Bring on the medics! Diagnosis — broken arm. Steve missed the medal-ceremony AND the F.A. Cup Final in May. He'll not forget his Wembley debut in a hurry!

. . . MUST COME DOWN!

GARY SPEED
Leeds United

OUT OF THE

DEAN HOLDSWORTH

(Wimbledon F.C.)

It was goals or bust for Dean Holdsworth last season.

Wimbledon owner Sam Hamman promised to reward his young striker with a sculpture in bronze if he scored enough goals last season. Not that the former Brentford player needed any extra incentive.

In his first season in the top flight, Holdsworth was determined to prove that he could be one of the most prolific goalscorers in the country. That's exactly what he'd done by the end of the season.

He finished up as third top scorer in the Premier League behind England strikers Teddy Sheringham and Les Ferdinand. His nineteenth and final goal came against champions Manchester United.

It was a year that also saw Dean finally step out from the shadow of his twin brother. Watford's David Holdsworth is Dean's biggest fan but last season he had to settle for playing Division One football.

"One day I hope Dave and I will be able to share Premier League success in the same team," says Dean.

"We both started our careers at Watford but I was never really given a chance there. The two of us actually played together as a centre-back partnership in the Watford reserves but that's about as far as we went together.

"While Dave established himself very quickly in the team, most of my appearances came as a sub or on loan to other clubs.

"I'm sure that we could do well together in the same team. As twins we share the same instincts and that's the sort of understanding that most managers are crying out for in a team.

"But I wouldn't want to play as a defender again like I did for Watford reserves. Scoring goals is a feeling you just can't beat.

"Perhaps one day I'll find him marking me. But he won't stop me from scoring!"

The twins have always been friends and follow each other's careers with great interest. When one gets injured, the other is quickly on the phone to check-up on the damage. Both have had their share of injuries in recent seasons — often at the same time.

It was only when he went to Brentford that things really started to happen for Dean. In a 110 league games he was to score 53 goals for the West London team, finally helping them

SHADOWS!

to win promotion from the old Division Three after years of trying.

Dean's 34 league and cup goals that season inevitably created interest amongst other clubs. It was Wimbledon who moved quickest to secure his services in a £725,000 deal.

The prospect of Dean playing alongside John Fashanu sounded like a certain source of goals for the Dons. But it didn't quite work out like that in the early months.

"Soon after I joined the club I developed a hernia problem," Dean explains. "I actually picked up the original injury in a pre-season friendly.

"It was so frustrating because I'd been very keen to make an immediate impression in the Premier League.

"Wimbledon had spent a lot of money on me and I wanted to show the club and the fans what I could do. I had to start repaying that money as quickly as possible.

"I'd been brought to the club to score goals and that's exactly what I intended doing. I knew it would be more difficult at a higher level but I wasn't going to let that worry me.

"I've always had confidence in my ability to score goals. If the chances are there, I will take them.

"I was actually quite pleased with my form and the goals I scored were certainly a bonus in those opening games. But all the time I was having to hide the injury.

"After the match I would be good for nothing. For days after all I could do was rest up for the next game.

"In the end, I had to bow to the inevitable. There was nothing else for it but to have the hernia operation.

"It proved to be a good decision. Although I didn't return to full fitness until January, it paid off with the goals I scored in the second half of the season.

"It was then that I got the chance to strike up a proper partnership with John Fashanu. Both of us like to get amongst defences and frighten them.

"That's exactly what happened towards the end of the season. Fash created havoc in the box and I picked up goals as result.

"There's nothing like scoring goals to make you feel better. I've always got a thrill from that ever since I played with David as a kid.

"There was even one occasion when Dave and I scored on the same day. I heard a shout from the crowd that he'd scored for Watford and that made me even more determined to score.

"I can't let him get one-up on me when it comes to goals. After all, Dave's job is defending — mine is scoring."

SNOW BALL!

Norwich City's Daryl Sutch and Ian Culverhouse dance it out with Jason Wilcox, Blackburn Rovers.

A STRI RESEMB

CHRIS KIWOMYA

CHRIS is rated one of the quickest strikers in the Premier League by breathless opposition defences.

The lightning pace of the Ipswich star earned him a huge reputation last season on his introduction to the top flight.

But quietly-spoken Chris was hiding an amazing secret — he's not as fast as his mum!

Kiwomya embarrasses top class defenders with his speed. But he was the most embarrassed of all when he was challenged by his mum to a race — and lost.

Mum, Curlyn, used to be the Jamaican sprint champion before settling in Yorkshire and producing footballing sons Andy and Chris.

As a teenager, Chris was the target for top league clubs like Leeds United and Sheffield Wednesday. He thought he was the bees-knees — but his mother thought he could do better.

"She said I wasn't trying hard enough," confesses Chris. "She took me to an athletics track and challenged me.

"I didn't think she was being serious. I thought I'd win easily. But she wanted to prove a point, so I ran against her.

"I ran as fast as I could, really put my foot down, but was amazed to find she could easily stay with me.

"I realised what was going to happen so I pulled up, pretending to be injured! I can laugh at it now, but it wasn't so funny at the time."

The experience taught Chris a valuable lesson. He began to work harder on his fitness and was signed as an apprentice by Ipswich.

It took him a few years to establish himself at Portman Road. But now Chris is one of the most highly-valued strikers in the game — thanks to mum.

Older brother, Andy, can also look back fondly at his childhood, although it's his DAD who gave him a lesson in running!

Dad Kiwomya used to place Andy, Chris and their brothers and sisters round a track, race them — AND beat them!

KING LANCE!

ANDY KIWOMYA

Comeback man Andy, another striker with a breathtaking burst of speed, found last season far tougher than he had ever anticipated — but the experience of helping Dundee secure Premier League survival did not sour him towards Scottish footbal.

"I felt under terrible pressure," said the 25-year-old.

"After five years out of the game I always knew I'd find it hard — but not as hard as it has been.

"Initially I had the worries of not knowing for sure that I could play again and whether or not my main asset, my pace, had gone because without my pace I'd be an ordinary player.

"And I've also had to cope with the pressure created by other people looking at the amount of goals my brother Chris has scored for Ipswich. They expected the same from me and the situation Dundee were in where the season was one long battle for points.

"All this meant I was unable to relax and enjoy my football fully. Although having gone through what I have, it's a price I was willing to pay just to be playing once more."

He continues, "Deep down I'd love to go back south again at some point and play against some of the lads — like Paul Ince, Michael Thomas and Neil Ruddock — who were team-mates in the England youth side.

"But for the moment I definitely want to stay with Dundee. The Scottish Premier League may be difficult but that makes it a challenge, and I like challenges."

Andy's career looked to have been finished when, in 1986, he suffered nerve and disc damage to his back in a training accident while with Sheffield Wednesday.

He embarked on a three year leisure management course at college and had a spell in the USA coaching.

"But not being able to do what I really wanted to made me depressed so I decided to have another go at playing and having tested myself in five matches for Frickley I felt encouraged enough to join Dundee," he said.

"Last season was all about buying time for the young players and trying to establish a team pattern while pursuing the points needed to stay up."

"ITS MINE!" "NO – IT'S MINE!"
Stoke City's Mark Stein and Steve Foley tussle for a loose ball.

CROSSWORD

ACROSS

1. This man gives TV/radio coverage of the game (11)
6. Number of players per side (6)
7. When the game is finished? (4)
8. Supporters (4)
10. Horizontal goal post (3)
12. The Hawthorns' West Bromwich. (6)
13. Elimination contest (3-3)
15. What any player must be (3)
16. Full time, to give out (4)
19. Visiting team (4)
20. Where matches take place (6)
21. Toshack's striking partner at Liverpool (5,6)

DOWN

1. Norwich, Stoke or Lincoln (4)
2. Italian city (5)
3. Three chances on the pools? (6)
4. A player from Bristol? (5)
5. This team knocked West Ham out of last season's FA Cup (8)
9. Take a kick at goal (5)
10. Manchester United's Steve (5)
11. Stars for Everton (4, 4)
14. Team from the Orient (6)
15. Mr McAvennie is honest! (5)
17. A road in Manchester (65)
18. This Mr Smith is a Gunner (5)

SEE 10 DOWN

WHO AM I?

A. I started my career with Newcastle United.

B. A move abroad saw me play on the losing side in the 1991 European Cup Final.

C. I'm now back home in England with a Premier League club. Our great city rivals are "The Blades".

ANSWERS

ACROSS
1 COMMENTATOR
6 ELEVEN 7 OVER 8 FANS
10 BAR 12 ALBION
13 CUP-TIE 15 FIT 16 EMIT
19 AWAY 20 STADIA
21 KEVIN KEEGAN.

DOWN
1 CITY 2 MILAN 3 TREBLE
4 ROVER 5 BARNSLEY
9 SHOOT 10 BRUCE
11 MARK WARD
14 LEYTON 15 FRANK
17 MAINE 18 ALAN

WHO AM I?
CHRIS WADDLE
(SHEFFIELD WEDNESDAY)

2 INTO 1 DOESN'T GO!

Southampton's IAIN DOWIE found that out!

I never really appreciated until last season what a lucky man I am to be playing professional football for a living.

Then I went with Northern Ireland to play a World Cup tie in Albania — and I saw how the other half live.

Albania is a beautiful country. Spectacular mountain scenery, wonderful views over the countryside.

But then you see the starving kids begging on the streets. Food is at a premium.

Albania is an oppressed country. The people have nothing. It's an eye-opener to visit a place like that.

It was quite upsetting. I returned home realising how well off I am, and what a lot I have going for me.

In actual fact I'm doubly lucky to be playing professional football. Without it I'd be out of a job.

I was a late arrival in league football. After leaving school I did an engineering apprenticeship, and got a job with British Aerospace.

Then I was spotted by Luton, playing for Hendon Town as a part-timer, and asked to sign as a pro. It was a pretty tough decision.

I had a good job in the defence industry. It seemed to offer more security than football.

I didn't know if I could make the grade as a footballer. In the end I decided I would regret it more if I didn't give myself the chance.

Things worked out quite well for me at Luton. But these days it looks an even better decision.

The factory I worked at has closed down. The defence side has gone. Most of my old mates are out of work.

I enjoyed working in the factory. But I've got to admit it's not the same as doing something you love for a living.

I can really appreciate now that I'm luckier than my old workmates, and much luckier than the poor people of Albania.

Because of that, I'm happy to work as hard as I can to make myself a better player. In the last year I've put in a lot of extra hours.

I go back in the afternoons to The Dell twice a week to work with the coaches and apprentices. I work on my shooting and passing, and technical skills.

Also, I watch as much Italian football on television as I can, to try to learn from players like Vialli. Certain things like his control and turning are brilliant.

I'm very interested in the different style of the Italian game. Ours is so much more physical, but we could learn a lot from them.

The extra work I put in last season helped me to win the first team spot at The Dell. The unfortunate thing was I had to take it from my best pal!

Before last season began, I was really looking forward to the start. I'd finished the previous year in good form, and had trained well.

But then the manager suddenly brought in Kerry Dixon from Chelsea, and Perry Groves from Arsenal. It was a bitter disappointment for me.

By coincidence, both Kerry and I owned houses in Luton that we couldn't sell. It made sense for us to travel down together for training, and occasionally share a hotel room.

Spending so much time together, Kerry and I became good pals. But that was all put aside when it came to football.

In the hours of driving up and down the motorways, Kerry and I talked football all the time. Obviously we discussed our own situations.

Kerry started off in the side, but I always thought I was good enough to be the number one. I knew that if I got a chance, I would have to take it with both hands.

We both knew we were fighting for one place — although our feeling was that we could do well together as a partnership, given the chance.

The gaffer didn't see it that way. We were never tried in the team together.

Obviously, competition for places is vital. We both understood it's important to have a strong squad. But every player wants to be a first-teamer.

When Kerry was injured early on, I came in and scored twice against Crystal Palace. Things went well for me after that, and Kerry couldn't get back in the side.

Eventually he went on loan to Luton, which was obviously convenient for him. Not so great for me — I had to do all the travelling on my own!

The Southampton fans were great to me last season. But I had to work hard to be accepted.

When I joined the club from West Ham, the fans were expecting a lot. I was one of the first signings by the new manager, Ian Branfoot.

Things didn't go too well for the team early on, so I was in the firing line. But I'm strong enough to accept that, and now I believe I've won them over.

They gave me a great reception last season, and I think all the disappointments are behind me.

The Dell is an imposing place for visiting teams these days. We're not an easy side to beat.

Everybody works hard. Even if I'm not scoring goals, I feel I'm contributing to the team.

But I'm looking forward to scoring a lot of goals this season. I know I'm a lucky man.

THE END OF A NIGHTMARE

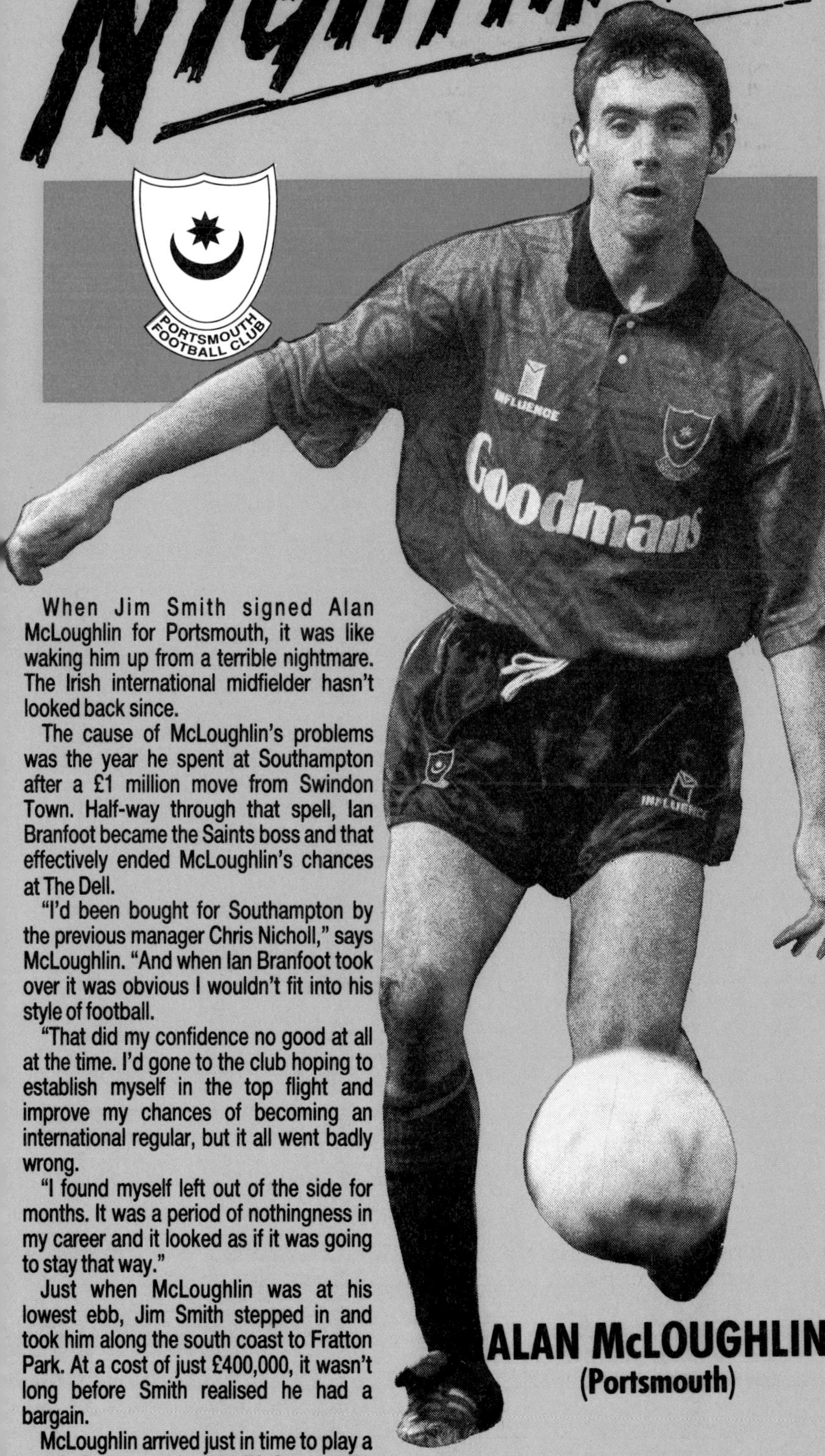

ALAN McLOUGHLIN
(Portsmouth)

When Jim Smith signed Alan McLoughlin for Portsmouth, it was like waking him up from a terrible nightmare. The Irish international midfielder hasn't looked back since.

The cause of McLoughlin's problems was the year he spent at Southampton after a £1 million move from Swindon Town. Half-way through that spell, Ian Branfoot became the Saints boss and that effectively ended McLoughlin's chances at The Dell.

"I'd been bought for Southampton by the previous manager Chris Nicholl," says McLoughlin. "And when Ian Branfoot took over it was obvious I wouldn't fit into his style of football.

"That did my confidence no good at all at the time. I'd gone to the club hoping to establish myself in the top flight and improve my chances of becoming an international regular, but it all went badly wrong.

"I found myself left out of the side for months. It was a period of nothingness in my career and it looked as if it was going to stay that way."

Just when McLoughlin was at his lowest ebb, Jim Smith stepped in and took him along the south coast to Fratton Park. At a cost of just £400,000, it wasn't long before Smith realised he had a bargain.

McLoughlin arrived just in time to play a part in Portsmouth's 1992 FA Cup run. He scored the winner against Nottingham Forest in the quarter-final and helped Pompey give Liverpool a hard time in the semi-final.

But McLoughlin and Portsmouth just missed out on Wembley — and the promotion play-offs as well. So last season they had to start again with the Premier League as their target.

It also gave McLoughlin the chance to play in the diamond formation he had first experienced under Ossie Ardiles at Swindon.

"Playing as the spearhead of a diamond formation is a role that suits my attacking style of play. But it's no easy option.

"It means I have to do a lot of running in a match shuttling between midfield and the front-two. And that all started to catch up with me last season.

"I started to cramp-up badly in my hamstrings during most games. It was probably as a result of the way I played, but I wasn't going to change that.

"But at the end of last season I had to be substituted in the latter stages of most games. I was always worried I was going to do some serious damage to the hamstring.

"That was the down-side of my position. The up-side was being just behind the prolific Guy Whittingham during his record-breaking season.

"With Guy around you always know something special is going to happen. He's one of the best finishers in the business.

"When you play the ball through to Guy, there's always a good prospect of a goal. He hates to waste chances.

"Scoring as many goals as he did last season was a wonderful achievement for any player. But he wasn't the only one to get amongst the goals because I got quite a few myself.

"And every goal I scored helped rebuild my confidence after the Southampton experience. Jim Smith must take much of the credit for that.

"He allowed me to play my best football again. Gradually, I could tell that I was returning to the sort of form I'd shown at Swindon."

That form made sure that McLoughlin stayed in Jack Charlton's Republic of Ireland squad as they tried to qualify for what would be his second World Cup. But he knew getting a place was a different matter.

"Even if you were playing in the Italian league, it would still be difficult to get a place in the Irish midfield. Andy Townsend, Ray Houghton, Roy Keane and Steve Staunton make it one of the best units in Europe.

"With that sort of competition around, I'm just happy to be in the squad. It's no disgrace to be kept out by class players like that."

PROMOTION was a matter of routine for West Ham's Peter Butler last season.

Before a match he'd take his two dogs off for a nice, long walk and give them both a pat on the head before he left for Upton Park. It became a superstition he kept to throughout last term.

Then, the midfield dynamo would recharge his batteries with a bowl of Bran Flakes and bananas as his pre-match meal. Just what he needed for ninety minutes of non-stop action.

"Walking the dogs and eating a bowl of cereal are just two of the habits I've got into on a match day," Peter admits. "And they worked out quite well for me last season.

"I've never been one to lie in bed of a match-day and worry. It's up and about for me to get some fresh air with the Labrador and the Retreiver. I love the outdoors and there's no better way of relaxing before a big game.

"My dogs don't care much about football but they know all about it when I've had a good game. They're always made a fuss of after we've won. I think they must have enjoyed last season nearly as much as me!

"I stick to the simple bowl of cereal and fruit before a match but I love to cook something more exciting in the evening. My wife is a qualified chef but I've picked up quite a few tips from her and now do most of it myself.

"My pre-match routine continues when I get to the ground. I always like to get out on to the pitch and have a good energetic warm-up. That gets me in just the right mood for the game itself.

"I get through a lot of running in a match so it's always very important that I'm properly warmed-up.

HABIT FORMING

Winning soon became another habit for West Ham's PETER BUTLER.

MISSED CONNECTION!

The ball flies past the combined challenge of Rangers' Alexei Mikhailichenko and Aberdeen duo Stephen Wright and Paul Mason.

"But I did once have an embarrassing experience when warming-up for a game for Huddersfield at Newcastle. It was very wet and I went flying on to my backside. The home fans gave me some stick for that."

Last season, Butler had Newcastle in his sights throughout the year as West Ham tried gallantly to catch Kevin Keegan's team in the Division 1 promotion race.

It was Butler's first campaign at Upton Park after his £170,000 transfer from Southend United. It was a move that owed as much to Billy Bonds' long memory as it did to Butler's form in the previous season.

He fully justified Bonds' faith in him, playing a full part in securing second place for the Hammers and finishing third in the club's Player-of-the Year award.

"I missed most of my last year at Southend with a ruptured tendon in my knee. It was a very disappointing way to end what had been a good time for me at the club.

"I'd played the best football of my career under David Webb. Sadly, it all fell apart for the club during my last year and I couldn't do much about it because of the injury.

"Thankfully, Billy knew that I'd had a decent season the year before and brought me to West Ham on the evidence of that.

"Things started off pretty well for me with the Hammers, until the injury jinx struck again in the November. I needed a double hernia operation and that knocked me out of the reckoning for a couple of months.

"That was very frustrating because Martin Allen and I had started to put a very good partnership together in the centre of midfield.

"Martin was a great inspiration to the team last season and I loved playing alongside him. We didn't score too many goals between us but I think we helped set up quite a few for the others."

Butler is a great competitior on the pitch and it's not surprising to discover that he was brought up on Rugby League in his native Halifax.

"I'd love to have played Rugby League. I used to go to watch Halifax as a kid and I've supported them ever since.

"But I also supported Leeds United, following them home and away as often as I could. So when I got the chance I became a football apprentice at Huddersfield instead of playing Rugby League. Later on I played for Bury and Cambridge, then Southend before joining West Ham.

"Having been a fan on the terraces myself in the past, I always make a point of saluting the supporters after a match. I know what they expect from the players.

"I always play better when the fans are right behind the team. That's exactly where the Hammers fans have been since I joined the club. They played a big part in our promotion campaign.

"Even when it looked as if automatic promotion was slipping away from us, they kept us going. Then on the last day they got their reward when we clinched our place in the Premier League.

"It had been quite a few weeks for me because my wife had just given birth to a baby boy. I'll get him playing Rugby League when he's older!

"There's no doubt that it has been here at West Ham that I've played my best football. This is the biggest of all the clubs I've been at and that's certainly inspired me.

"The combination of Billy Bonds and Harry Redknapp has worked wonders for me. It didn't take them long to make me a better player than I'd ever been."

DAVID WHITE
Manchester City

FRANCO BARESI
A.C. Milan

The Record NO

When I eventually come to look back on my playing career I hope it won't be summed up by the words 'missed opportunities'. Up to now, that's how I describe it. But in the next few years I hope to enjoy greater success.

LAST season was typical of my career. A lot of promise, a lot of potential, but in the end not amounting to very much. For example, in the space of 20 minutes last season I achieved the greatest ambition of my career — and also the biggest disappointment of my life.

It was all to do with playing for England. For the first time I was selected for the senior England squad, for the friendly match against Spain in Santander.

Obviously I hoped to be on from the start, but instead I was named among the subs. Before the interval, Graham Taylor told me I would be going on for the second half.

I felt great. Couldn't wait for the second half to start. An England cap at long last. All I could think of was that I had 45 minutes in which to make a real impression, and show what I could do at international level. I'd waited a long time for the chance.

But in my very first challenge for the ball I damaged my ankle. There was no way I could carry on. I was gutted. It was hard to drag myself off the pitch. I had played only 18 minutes of international football.

I couldn't believe it. I'm very rarely injured. Before that I'd missed only one match in three seasons for QPR — and that was from a sore throat.

But by an unbelievable coincidence, when I played for the England Youth team, I had to come off with the same sort of ankle injury. There must be some sort of jinx on me.

It's a bit heartbreaking. I just hope I don't go into the record books as having the shortest international career of all time. I'd love another chance.

I suppose I should be pleased at

-ONE wants to break!

by DAVID BARDSLEY Q.P.R.

getting on the field and earning an England cap. I am proud of that. I'm as pleased for my father as for myself. He has always been a great support to me.

My dad was a top amateur player who won England caps, and represented the army. He was always a big influence on me.

When I was a youngster, and attached to Coventry City, it was my dad who did all the fetching and carrying. Winning my first cap was a reward for him and my mum.

I was beaten to the cap by my boyhood pal Paul Stewart, who was picked a year earlier by Graham Taylor while he was playing for Spurs.

Paul and I grew up together in Manchester. We were in the same boys team, and worked together in the market.

We played for a Sunday League side which was so strong that eight of the boys went on to join League clubs. Paul and I went to Blackpool as apprentices.

He was a striker, and already had an unbelievable work-rate up front — but he scored very few goals.

It took a long time for Paul to be switched into midfield, which has proved to be his best position. Once he did drop back, he won his England cap within a year.

Paul and I both made our debuts for Blackpool at the age of 17 — he beat me again by three months — and established ourselves in the first team together.

But we were split up when I was signed by Watford. The manager, of course, was Graham Taylor.

In my first season we reached the final of the FA Cup — and defeat by Everton became the first of my missed opportunities.

We'd had two mega games against Everton in the League that year, one of them an amazing 4-4 draw. But at Wembley we just didn't get going.

It was very disappointing. We were very poor. But I'd got to Wembley at a very young age — only 19 — and I always thought I would have another chance.

So far it hasn't happened — but I will keep hoping. I know I should have made the most of it at the time.

In fact I came very close to missing out altogether on Wembley. I developed a dodgy knee in training about three weeks before the final. A few days before the match I was convinced I wouldn't play. But Watford gave me every chance.

I had burst a capsule behind the knee, and the day before the match the doctor drained it. They took about a pint of blood.

I was lucky. I passed a fitness test and played at Wembley. But it was so nearly another missed opportunity.

Before I joined Watford, I was wanted by Manchester City — Paul Stewart did eventually go there — but nothing came of it. And while I was at Watford, Graham Taylor turned down a bid for me from Arsenal.

I always felt that a move to a big name club might have helped me make an earlier breakthrough to international level.

Selection for England is very much a matter of opinion and luck. But it must help to be playing for one of the very big clubs.

It was very frustrating to be overlooked year after year. I think I might have been picked much earlier in my career if I had been with one of the 'fashionable' clubs.

No disrespect to anyone. But I have faith in my own ability. I believe I have been one of the best right-backs in the country for the last three or four years.

When Graham Taylor was appointed England manager, I hoped that might be in my favour. He knew what I could do from my Watford days. Graham has always favoured players that he has known from club management. Perhaps in the end it did help me get into the squad.

However, I know I'm a far better defender now than when I was with him at Watford. I've progressed a lot in the last few years.

At Watford I was always better going forward. In fact Graham Taylor played me as a right-winger for a spell. Attacking down the wing, and getting in crosses, was the strongest part of my game. But with help from first Don Howe, and then Gerry Francis, at Rangers, I've worked hard on my defensive play.

Defending is now my strength. I enjoy the challenge of playing against the top wingers because I usually do well against them.

Gerry Francis has done a tremendous job at QPR. It's no coincidence that Les Ferdinand and Andy Sinton have also won England caps since he took over.

We have the potential to become one of the top clubs in the country. I just hope it won't become another missed opportunity.

ANDY MUTCH
Wolves

ANDY TOWNSEND
Chelsea

ANDY IMPEY
Queens Park Rangers

LEE HURST
Coventry City

RANGERS'
STUART McCALL

AN ELLAND

EVERYTHING changed very quickly for me at the beginning of season 1991-92 — but looking back it was the best move I could have made.

Things hadn't been going too well at Everton, where I wasn't holding down a regular first-team place, so I was quite keen to move on.

I'd known that Rangers were interested in me during the close-season, but nothing had come of it and I'd prepared myself for another season at Goodison.

ROAD FIRST!

Any move to Ibrox was dependent on Marseille signing Trevor Steven, and that deal looked to have fallen through when he played the first couple of games of the season.

But suddenly the deal was back on and within a couple of days I found myself stepping straight into Trevor's shoes while he went to Marseille.

Unfortunately, my introduction to life as a Rangers player was anything but smooth.

After negotiations between Ibrox boss Walter Smith and Howard Kendall at Everton, I was signed for £1.2 million on the Friday, and given the all-clear to play against Hearts at Tynecastle on the Saturday.

But I had hardly put a Rangers jersey on for the first time when we were a goal down. Scott Crabbe scored for the home side after only 90 seconds — and we ended up losing 1-0.

I found myself chasing the ball all over the park, yet hardly getting a look in as the action raged on around me.

Although it was a far from ideal start, I can honestly say that I haven't looked back since.

During that season, Rangers went on to win the League and Cup double — their first since 1978 — celebrating their first Scottish Cup victory in 11 years.

And I got an immediate idea of the size of support Rangers enjoy in a Skol Cup game against Queen's Park on the Tuesday night following the Hearts game.

At Everton, a comparable fixture might have been against a lower division side, such as Rochdale, and you might expect a crowd of 9,000 or so to turn up.

But for my home debut there was a staggering 32,000 there, and I just couldn't believe the noise when I walked down the tunnel.

Thankfully, there were no hiccups this time and we ran out 6-0 winners.

Since then everything's gone like a dream for me at Ibrox.

Having played at Everton, I wouldn't have believed people could be any more fanatical about their football than they are on Merseyside — until I came to Glasgow!

Rangers' deadly double act — Ally McCoist and Mark Hateley

Everywhere I go I'm recognised and talked to, but thankfully I've never had any hassle.

Part of my family live near Glasgow, in Hamilton, and they are all Rangers supporters, so that made it easier for me to settle in.

I knew the city quite well anyway, with trips up north as a boy and then through involvement with the Scotland squad. It's a place I really like, and my wife and children all enjoy life here.

As far as playing is concerned, there's certainly been no lack of highlights since I made my move to Ibrox.

But if I had to pick a favourite game, it would have to be the Scottish Cup semi-final against Celtic last March.

At that time, to beat them 1-0 was the best result of my career. The odds were stacked against us after our full-back David Robertson was sent off early on in the first half.

But somehow we managed to weather the storm, and Ally McCoist scored to send us through to the final — when we won against Airdrie.

It would have been difficult to believe I could ever have topped that game. But last season turned out to be even better.

It's well known that as a youngster I supported Leeds. So to get the chance to play against them with Rangers in the European Cup — and beat them both home and away — was really special for me.

After the first leg at Ibrox, which we won 2-1, the English media still expected Leeds to go through.

And I had never won a game at Elland Road, so to go there and prove that Rangers were the strongest team in Britain was fantastic.

Since then the spotlight has been firmly on Ibrox, from the whole of Britain, and that can only be good for the club.

Every player wants to be involved in big games, and there's been no shortage of them since I came here. My only worry has been that the number of games we're forced to play will take its effect on our form.

As a boy I remember supporting Leeds when they won the FA Cup against Arsenal in 1972, then had to play the Championship decider against Wolverhampton just 48 hours later — which they lost.

With a 44-game league in Scotland, it doesn't take long before the games start piling up, especially if your team is successful in domestic or European cup competitions.

All that can take its toll, but at Rangers we have a big enough squad to cope fairly well — although I enjoy my summer breaks more than ever these days!

In retrospect my move north has been great, from the point of view of playing for both club and country.

I would never have been involved in so many big games if I'd stayed with Everton, so I have to be happy — and hope that long may it continue!

JOHN BYRNE
Millwall

RAY HOUGHTON
Aston Villa

MAKE

BY JIM BEGLIN

PHOTOGRAPH COURTESY OF CORK EXAMINER

IN football terms, the transition made by Jim Beglin is something akin to being a gamekeeper-turned-poacher.

In a career which seems destined to reap a collection of medals, he earned only one League Championship medal, and an FA Cup winner's gong with Liverpool, plus 15 international caps for the Republic of Ireland, before he was cruelly forced to retire through injury just as he was approaching his prime.

Now the 30-year-old maintains an interest in the game from the other side of the fence. Instead of playing, he earns his money on a Saturday afternoon by donning his earphones and wielding a microphone as he sends his Premier League match reports over the airwaves to radio listeners nationwide.

He has also turned his hand to writing since he started doing a twice-weekly column for an Irish newspaper and is aiming to build a successful career as a football journalist.

Nevertheless, he still finds it difficult to reconcile himself to the fact that a promising playing career was cut short so painfully.

Says Jim, "I should probably be in my prime just now. I was only 23 when I sustained the broken leg which was finally to force my retirement.

"By then, I had started to command a regular place in the Liverpool side and I was Jack Charlton's number one left back in the Republic side. I really thought I had everything going for me.

"I was heartbroken when it all ended. For whatever reason, I would never have chosen to leave Liverpool. If I had my way, I'd still be there now."

It was in a League Cup match against local rivals Everton that he shattered his left leg.

"The date was January 21, 1987 — that will be etched on my mind for ever," he recalls. "Unfortunately, it's the moment in my career that I seem to be remembered for.

"It seems a long time ago now, yet I'll probably never be allowed to forget it."

Years of painful rehabilitation and a failed comeback followed before Beglin was forced to quit.

He goes on, "The leg didn't knit together well for a while and I was in a full leg plaster for so long that all the components in my leg had to be taught how to work again. I virtually had to learn how to walk properly once more.

"It was 18 months before I played in a reserve match, but despite a spell of pre-season training prior to the next campaign, I still wasn't running correctly.

"It was soon obvious that I wasn't going to get back into the Liverpool first team. They gave me a free transfer, which was a nice gesture because they could have asked for a few quid and made it awkward for me.

"Leeds United manager Howard Wilkinson signed me. It was brilliant of him to give me a chance, because he knew he was taking a big risk. The whole thing was a nightmare in the end. After getting over something so bad, my right knee also played up. Things just dragged on and eventually I had to quit.

"At that stage, I didn't know what on earth I was going to do. I had few qualifications to fall back on. I'd passed my examinations at school, but never concentrated on anything in particular. Football was my life at that stage.

"Two weeks after leaving school, I was doing pre-season training at Shamrock Rovers with Johnny Giles when he was trying to establish a professional team.

"But he also liked to encourage his youngsters to think about their futures, and tried to persaude me to take a college course.

"They sent me to do a pre-University course, but when I arrived there I found it was like an advanced version of the Leaving Certificate I'd gained at school — the equivalent of an A-level in England. I decided I didn't want to go through all that again, so I dropped out to devote all my time to football.

"Having experienced the pain and heartbreak of having to give up early, I'd now advise any kid to get whatever qualifications he can. If you can get something behind you, it's absolutely brilliant to have a course to fall back on at the end of your playing career.

"When it all ended at Leeds, I sat in manager Howard Wilkinson's office, without a clue about what to do, when he asked me, 'What about your radio work?'"

At that stage, I was doing little bits of reporting for RTE, the Irish radio and television network.

"It had started shortly after I broke my leg, when I was unable to play for the Irish team. When international week came around, they had asked me if I fancied sitting in on a couple of commentary games as a summariser.

"I did so, it went OK, and they asked me to do some more.

"Sure enough, Howard Wilkinson's suggestion began to bear fruit. After I'd retired, RTE asked if I'd like to move up from summarising to reporting.

"At first I wasn't sure if I was cut out for it, because I knew that summarising was a lot easier. In that job, the commentator does all the hard work, while I'd just have to sit there and make observations as the match went along.

"However, I agreed to have a go, and soon found it OK. It was harder because basically you're on the spot when the link-man hands over to you. It's not so bad if he leads in with a question and gives you something to talk about. I could go on all day then. But when he simply cues you in by saying, 'Over to Jim Beglin', that's it. You need your own introduction, and may have to talk for a minute or so.

YOURSELF HEARD!

"At first I was scripting a lot. I'd simply read from my text, and try to make it sound as if it was coming from the top of my head.

"Now I find it's getting easier. I just scribble a couple of notes to help me get through. It pleases me to be improving like that, because I'd like to reach the stage where it all comes spontaneously.

"On a Saturday, I generally cover a Premier League match for an RTE channel show which mixes sport, music and chat. There's a lot of racing, but quite a big spot for English football.

"The audience for the game on this side of the water is fantastic. Though the League of Ireland is a reasonable standard and a good base for young players just starting out, everybody looks to English football as their big interest, and the support a lot of the clubs receive from Ireland is fantastic.

"I don't always look for the Irish angle in the match I'm covering, but if something happens to an Irish player, then I'll highlight it. For instance, Kevin Moran broke his nose in a clash with Justin Fashanu in last season's Blackburn v Wimbledon match, so that was important to the Irish.

"I'm still at the learning stage, and don't think I'll ever make a brilliant journalist, but I enjoy the reporting, and I've had a good reaction from listeners. People regularly stop me to say they enjoy my reports.

"I don't know whether I was ever going to be the right material for football coaching or management, as I think you have to be ruthless, and I'm a bit too nice for that game.

"So reporting has been a good way of keeping in touch with the game. I still mix with the lads and go on trips to big matches. It's lovely to stay involved.

"I cover most of the Republic's matches, and I get myself on to the pitch as soon as the final whistle blows. I started it in Copenhagen after the lads had played against Denmark last season, continued it in Spain at the next World Cup qualifying match, and hope to be able to do so after all the matches.

"I just grab a couple of the lads as they are coming off the field and chat away.

"I found it a little bit awkward at first. I don't want to run onto the pitch with a pair of headphones and a mike, expecing them to speak just because I've played with them. But so far, they've been absolutely brilliant.

"Sometimes, if it has been a tough match, it's the last thing a player wants to do. So if anybody was to say, 'No, Jim' — I'd understand completely.

"As a former player, I know every player feels at times that the Media don't always handle things the way they would like. But now I'm seeing both sides of the argument.

"The Media is obviously a very powerful force in its own way. It can do a lot of harm, or a lot of good depending on how it is used.

"If nice things are being said in the papers or on the TV and radio about a player, then there's no problem. But everybody has an off-day and sometimes there is a need to say that. But as soon as you do, there is going to be trouble.

"Whenever I took stick in the paper, I was always scowling and unhappy. Really it should be accepted as part of the job."

During the past year, Beglin has expanded his duties to include writing.

He explains, "Just after the start of last season, an Irish newspaper asked me if I'd like to write a twice-weekly football column.

"My Monday piece generally revolves around the match I'd watched on the Saturday. Having seen a lot of different teams, I can highlight their good and bad points, and what I think of their prospects.

"The remainder of my work consists of comments on what has been happening in the football world.

"I try to steer away from controversy, but if a big story comes up, I'll offer my opinion. For instance, I aired my views about the Vinny Jones video last year.

"My busiest time is on an international night. I still do my summarising, then my after-match interviews. Then I'll probably take part in a panel discussion for radio before writing a piece for the following morning's paper.

"It's still on a casual basis and I have plenty of time for golf. But it would be nice if somebody offered me a staff job eventually."

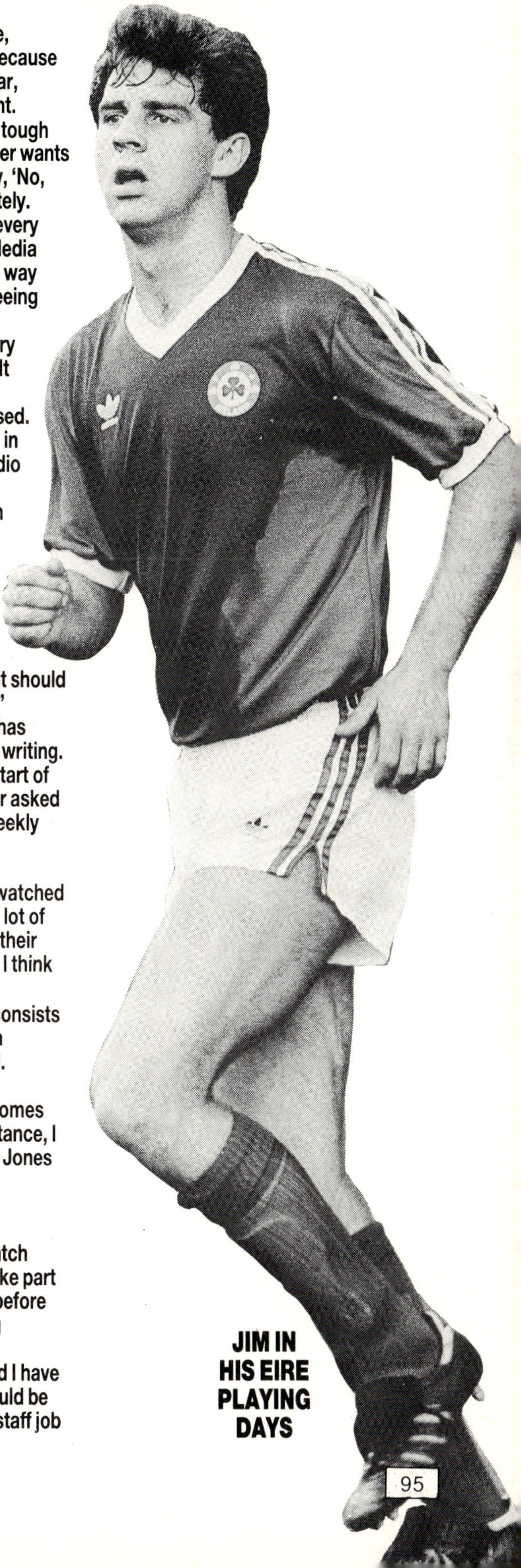

JIM IN HIS EIRE PLAYING DAYS

WHERE DID IT GO? Blackburn's **ALAN SHEARER** battles for a high ball with Arsenal's **TONY ADAMS.**

MARCO GABBIADINI
Derby County

THE GEORDIE GENIUS

THE STORY OF GAZZA

Paul Gascoigne . . . like him, or loathe him, he's one of the best players England has produced for many years. This is the story of his rise from obscurity to international fame . . .

Gazza came back to England a national hero and later on that year became only the second footballer to win the coveted BBC Sports Personality of the Year, pipping snooker's Stephen Hendry and cricketer Graham Gooch.
BBC
Season 90-91 saw Spurs reach the FA Cup semi-final. Only London rivals Arsenal stood in their way of a Cup Final appearance. The White Hart Lane side won 3-1 with Gazza scoring from a spectacular free-kick.
Unfortunately, the Final itself was a personal tragedy for Gazza. A reckless tackle saw the end of his involvement — and possibly the end of his career — due to a horrendous knee injury.
S.S LAZIO
Already linked with Italian giants Lazio for £8.5 m this move was put on ice while specialists debated his continued involvement in soccer.
After a long rehabilitation and training programme, the transfer was eventually completed and he made his first appearance for Lazio on 25th September, 1992.
The Lazio fans had two months to wait, though, before they saw Gazza's first league goal for the club. He couldn't have picked a better occasion — the equaliser in the derby with Roma! Gazza had arrived!
The glamour and big wages in Italy haven't led Gazza to forget his roots. He still has time to pop home — for a spot of fishing on Tyneside . . .
Paul Gascoigne, the Geordie lad who made good . . . rubbing shoulders with the cream of world soccer — and loving every minute of it!
BANCA DI ROMA

STEVE THOMPSON
Leicester City

CHRIS BART-WILLIAMS
Sheffield Wednesday

UNITED F

MARK ROBINS stood on the Old Trafford terraces as a lad. He's still one of their greatest fans. Yet last season Robins came close to dishing out United's greatest humiliation.

He scored the goals that could have won Norwich City the Premier League title — after Manchester United had virtually given him away to their rivals.

An ambition realised. Mark in United colours.

In the end, Norwich's leaky defence cost them the chance to win the title, after they had been firmly in the driving seat with a nine point lead.

The season ended in disappointment for Robins and Norwich. They tailed off after leading the table for much of the season, up to the last month.

But the consolation for the striker was that his beloved Reds finally won the championship after a wait of 26 years.

And his personal goalscoring record for Norwich established him firmly as a top-class finisher.

The disappointment was that Robins had to leave Old Trafford to prove a point. He was never really given the chance to establish a regular place for United.

"It was a wrench for me to leave Manchester United. A real tough decision," reveals Robins.

"I've lived up there all my life, and always supported United. All I ever wanted to do was to play for the Reds.

"Manchester United is a great club. I'll always be a fan.

"But as a professional footballer you have to think of your career. I had come to the stage when I had to get first team football.

"At Old Trafford I just wasn't getting a regular place. I spent a lot of time on the subs bench.

"Often I'd get on for five or ten minutes, then be out again. I wasn't playing enough matches.

"Sometimes I didn't play at all for two weeks. I lost match fitness, and I lost the chance to improve.

"You can only learn from playing football, and I wasn't getting enough chances to do that.

"When I did play, I was quite pleased with the way I performed for United. I think I managed 17 first team goals in about 25 starts .

"But I didn't start enough first team games, and I knew I had to move on to establish myself in the game.

"I could have stayed another year at Old Trafford, because I was still under contract to United. But I didn't want any more frustration at sitting on the sidelines.

"When it came to joining Norwich City, a few of my mates said things like 'where's Norwich?' They tried to make out it was too far out of the way.

"But I love it. It's a beautiful part of the world. I certainly didn't see it as a gamble."

Robins began his Norwich career in great style, coming off the bench to score twice on his debut.

In no time he had rattled in ten league goals to put Norwich at the top, and leave United trailing. Perhaps only an ankle injury, which put Mark out for five games, saved Alex Ferguson from serious embarrassment.

There are people who thought the selection of Robins might have won United the Championship the previous year. Ferguson's team was chronically short of goals on the run-in, and were pipped at the post by Leeds.

Manager Ferguson ignored the young striker, and Robins could only sit on the sidelines, full of frustration, as United blew their championship chance.

"I can't speculate about what might have happened. It's all water under the bridge," says Mark.

"I'm a Norwich player now, and enjoying myself at Carrow Road."

Robins did pick up an FA Cup winners medal in 1990, as substitute in the 3-3 draw again Palace, and again in the replay.

He had played a major part in getting United to Wembley, scoring three vital goals, including the semi-final winner.

Robins' early experience with United was alongside Mark Hughes

OR EVER!

— the player who was his hero when he was a young fan on the terraces.

"It felt weird to be sharing the same pitch as Mark Hughes. I must admit I was overawed at first," admits Mark.

"I could never be the kind of player that Mark Hughes is. It would be impossible for me to emulate the kind of things he does.

"I have to develop my own assets. But I have tried to learn from players like Mark in the hope that I can be as successful.

"My first few months with Norwich was the best spell I've had in first team football. It was great to score some goals for Norwich to justify their faith in me.

"But although it's my job to score goals, I don't mind not scoring as long as the team is doing well. I think I have other strengths as well.

"I don't think I get much credit for my all-round game. I have assets in my game other than goalscoring.

"People have said I don't play outside the box. But it takes a lot of hard work to earn your space to score goals.

"I believe I have a good football brain. I know when and where to make my runs.

"I don't think it's fair to label me as just a goal-poacher. I play my part in the build-up.

"You have to remember I've only had one full season in first team football, so I still have a lot to learn."

Ultimately Robins hopes to be one of the first graduates of the FA School of Excellence to win a full England cap.

"I'm not even thinking in terms of international football yet. I've got a long way to go before that," he says.

"But obviously it's everybody's ambition to play for England. I am no different.

"Apart from Alan Shearer, most of the possible England strikers are around the age of 26 or even older. That gives me a bit of time to develop.

"I hope I can continue to improve with Norwich. It is a very good club, even if it's a lot different to Manchester United.

"The pressures are much less at Norwich. Everything is very intense at Old Trafford. The expectations are so high.

"The fans expect United to win every match, and that puts pressure on the players. At United you feel that if you don't win about 3-0, it's a crisis!

"Things are different at Norwich. The fans want to win, but they don't expect quite so much. I enjoy it at Carrow Road."

RONALD KOEMAN
Barcelona

MARK STEIN
Stoke City

UTILITY MAN

THAT'S LIVERPOOL'S STEVE McMANAMAN

AFTER their shock FA Cup third round exit at the hands of Second Division Bolton Wanderers in January, Liverpool couldn't wait for last season to end.

A lowly league position and early exits from both major Cup competitions meant that Liverpool were faced with the rare situation of finishing the season playing for nothing more than pride.

Their boss and former Liverpool player, Graeme Souness, will not appreciate being reminded that it was the Reds' most traumatic season since the 1950s.

Injuries to key players such as Ronnie Whelan, Steve Nicol, David Burrows and Jan Molby tested their depth of squad and put the onus on Anfield's young guns and they didn't let their boss down.

It was a major test of character for 21-year-olds Steve McManaman and Don Hutchison, and 19-year-old Jamie Redknapp. And while they all passed the test with flying colours, it was McManaman who impressed.

The winger broke into the Liverpool first-team in season 1990-91, but it was last season when he firmly established himself as a key member of Souness's plans to recapture the club's glory days.

Although he was one of the most inexperienced players, he showed a maturity beyond his years last season. And while many of the senior members of the side suffered loss of form, McManaman was one of the most consistent performers.

"If there's a big difference between my performances last season and the season I broke into the side, it must be in terms of consistency," Steve says. "I feel I'm now a more consistent player, therefore a more reliable player.

"During my first season in the first-team my inexperience was there for everyone to see. I'd play well in one game and then be quiet for the next four or five. Of course, I still can't turn it on every week, but at least I'm doing it most weeks.

"When I was dropped the season before last I didn't feel I needed a rest. Although I felt physically fine the boss probably felt it was getting to me

Steve gets to grips with Norway's Steiner Nilsson during last year's U-21 international.

emotionally. In that respect I feel I grew up a lot last term.

"Nothing was handed on a plate last season. The results didn't go our way and I had a couple of niggling injuries which could have unsettled me.

"I had hamstring then groin trouble earlier in the season which forced me to miss a couple of games. In the past it would probably have knocked me out my stride, but not last season.

"There's been a lot of chopping and changing to the side. I've been asked to play alongside different players and it's never easy trying to strike up an understanding right away. However, I've approached it with a positive attitude."

McManaman has added the 'utility' tag to his list of accomplishments. He believes it presents a better opportunity for him to safeguard his future at Anfield.

"I played right and left midfield, as well as upfront last season," he goes on. "It's something the boss is keen for me to work hard on.

"It's all very well being a reliable winger or striker, but the modern game demands that players like myself are able to switch positions if needed.

"The injury situation we've had at Liverpool over the past year or so has made it crucial that players can fit in to different roles. No one can afford to be a one-dimensional player at Liverpool.

"Players like John Barnes, Mark Walters, Mike Marsh, Don Hutchison and myself can all play at least a couple of positions, and we've all been forced to do so at various stages. We must have the most flexible midfield in the country.

"It's reached the stage where if the boss was to ask me to be an emergency right-back I'd do it without question. I'm not saying I'd particularly enjoy it, but I'd be fairly confident of doing a decent job.

"I've spent a lot of time in training working on defensive aspects to my game. In the past I concentrated on going forward, but I'm developing an all-round game.

"There's still a lot of work to do, and I don't find it easy to concentrate on defensive duties when I'm not used to it.

"I'm also trying to improve my heading ability. I was stuck on the wing for much of my early time in the side and heading the ball was the least of my worries. But now I'm moving about more I'm getting more chances to head the ball."

Steve was awarded the captaincy of the England U-21 side towards the end of last season. In his first match at the helm he got off to a winning start beating San Marino 6-0 in a World Cup qualifier.

It's clear that the coach, Lawrie McMenemy, believes he's now acquired a sense of responsibility to go in tandem with his natural ability.

And as McManaman admits, the honour of captaining his country is thanks to the experience he's gathered during turbulent times at Anfield.

"Ian Hendon of Spurs was the captain against Turkey. But Ian wasn't picked for the squad to face San Marino and all the players were wondering who would get the nod.

"I must admit I didn't put myself down as favourite to get the job. It could have been any of us. I thought at the time Lawrie might go for my Anfield team-mates Rob Jones or Jamie Redknapp.

"When he pulled me out the line and told me I was captain I was surprised. I'm not really a natural leader. The last time I was captain of any team was at Campion High School in Everton five or six years ago.

"To be honest, I don't think it would have mattered too much who was captain that night. It wasn't the toughest match I was involved in last season, but it was still a great honour.

"I think my experience at Liverpool could have been decisive. I've now played nearly 100 games in the last couple of years and that's a lot of experience for a 21-year-old.

"I'm in the lucky position to have experienced more in my short career than some players do in their whole career. It's not something I've taken for granted.

"The boss says he picks players on merit, not reputations. That's how I got in the team in the first place. I know I've got to keep producing the goods or risk being dropped. It's as simple as that."

"OUCH! That hurt!" The expression says it all as Aston Villa's **PAUL McGRATH** gets the better of **DAVID WHITE**, Manchester City.

BRIAN LAUDRUP
Fiorentina

LIGHTNING STRIKES

COVENTRY CITY'S John Williams is the fastest man in English football. But after a long chase Bobby Gould finally managed to catch him.

Williams is the kind of attacking player defenders have nightmares about. As well as being frighteningly quick, he has a knack for scoring spectacular goals.

But it's the pace of the 24-year-old ex-postman which first catches the eye. That speed played a big part in helping him climb from the obscurity of Sunday League football to the big time with Premier League Coventry.

After having his eye on the player for some time, Gould eventually got his man in August '92 by paying Swansea £250,000 for their star forward.

The move capped a marvellous few months for John, who had won the Rumbelows Sprint Challenge final at Wembley in April, despite suffering from asthma.

He takes up the story, "I thought the Sprint Challenge was a joke at first — until I found out about the £10,000 first prize.

"I had a bad groin strain when the gaffer nominated me, so I didn't think it could be all that serious. He told me just to go off to the area heats in Portsmouth, enjoy the day out and to bring back the money and he would do the rest!

"When I got to Portsmouth everyone was talking about Michael Gilkes of Reading as the favourite. No-one knew who I was. A steward stopped me at the door and said, 'Who are you?' I told him and he said, 'Have you ever done any running before?' I told him only on Saturdays!

"But I won the first heat and beat Michael in the final. They started to take notice then because my odds went down from 50-1 to 20-1. Looking back, I wish I'd had a bet on myself!

"When the day of the final came, all the lads at Swansea put money on me to win, even though they really didn't believe I would. We ended up winning about £1100 on those bets!

"In the final itself, I got off to a bad start because I didn't hear the gun. I just stood up and started going. I hoped I could catch them by halfway because then I knew I could win.

"Luckily, I caught up with them and started to pull away in the lead — and there was ten grand in the bank!

"The thing is, because nobody at the club thought I would win, they said if I did I could keep the money . . . it's still there now!

"It was amazing. I had just come from being a postman and playing non-League football. I had never seen anything like that kind of money.

"Of course, a lot of people now say that I made my name from the Sprint Challenge. That might be true, but I also want to be known for my football.

"I wouldn't say winning it has had any bearing on my career. How many footballers actually run 100 metres at a time in a match? Football is all about running small distances.

"Look at Micky Gynn. He'll beat me any day over 10 yards, but any distance after that I'll thrash him. To be honest, as long as I play well I'm not bothered about how fast I am.

"But if the Sprint Challenge comes up again I'll definitely want to enter. It was good fun."

Following his astonishing first season as a professional, it is ironic to think that Williams nearly gave up the game for good when he was a child.

A bad experience while playing for his junior side soured him against football. For over four years John didn't kick a ball.

"When I was 15 I played in a junior cup semi-final for my team. I came on as sub and made all our goals. But when it came round to the final I didn't even get a shirt.

"I was only a young lad and the experience upset me. The team won the cup and I was gutted to think I'd done well in the semis and wasn't played in the final.

"In my later teens I used to play on and off for Newton Albion — the same club that Carlton Palmer played for. The manager would always phone me up on Sundays and ask me if I fancied a game. If I wasn't doing anything I'd say OK.

"What changed my mind about football was the fact that I was getting bored. I was working all the time and I needed something in my life to fill the gap. And I got really fed-up of getting up at 4.30 in the morning!

"Anyway, the Newton Albion boss was the chief scout at Shrewsbury. I remember him telling me years ago that I had a lot of potential and I could go a long way if I took it more seriously. At the time I didn't think anything of it.

"A while later, one of my mates went for a trial with non-League Cradley Town and he had my boots in the back of his car. When we got there he was egging me to play too, but I didn't want to.

"The manager saw this and asked me if I was any good. I told him I was alright and he persuaded me to have a go.

"When the game finished I think he had pound signs flashing in his eyes! He got me to sign a contract right there and then.

"I was so naive I thought, 'Getting paid to play football? Wow!', so like an idiot I signed it. A year and a half later they sold me to Swansea."

Before the move to Swansea, John had actually been spotted by Bobby Gould, then the manager of West Bromwich Albion.

"There were a lot of managers looking at the lads in our team," says Williams. "I knew Bobby was at the ground but I thought he was looking at my mate John Ford, who now plays for Swansea.

"During the game I got an attack of cramp. I went off for a couple of minutes, stretched my legs until it eased, came back on and scored a beauty from 25 yards!

"The minute I'd done that the cramp came back and I started limping again. Bobby probably thought, 'He's just a poser.'

"I didn't hear anything from West Brom for a while and Swansea were showing definite interest, so I signed for them.

"While I was playing for them we visited the Hawthorns to play West Brom. We were 2-0 down with 12 minutes left and came back to win 3-2.

"Stephen Thornber got a hat-trick and I set-up all his goals. After that I think Bobby Gould made up his mind to get me one way or the other!

"I heard he made a bid while I was at Vetch Field, but Swansea turned him down. I'm glad he kept me in mind when he went to Coventry and gave me a chance to play in the Premier League."

NG

S!

BY COVENTRY CITY'S JOHN WILLIAMS

KEVIN BALL
Sunderland

A KNUCKLE SANDWICH!
Ian Bryson, Sheffield United, gets his teeth into a challenge with Leeds United's Chris Whyte

THE GOOD

WHY a sudden return to the long shorts of bygone days? And why have some clubs gone digging into the distant past for ideas for new strips? Perhaps the answer lies in a Leeds city centre office, headquarters of Arkwright Clothing.

Tottenham Hotspur didn't only cause a stir, they also started a fashion when they turned out for the 1991 FA Cup Final wearing knee-length shorts.

A similar stir affected football when Manchester United launched their now famous green and yellow third strip, similar to the kit once worn by their ancestral predecessors, Newton Heath.

Old-fashioned soccer strips have become big business and it's all down to Arkwright, a four-year-old firm who manufacture strips from days of yore. Fans not too impressed by the silky, gaudy kits of today have found a friend in the heavy, cotton garments of the 1960's.

Back then it wasn't shadow stripes, sponsors' logos or flashy designs that distinguished one kit from another. Instead it was usually little more than the colours.

Arkwright, a brand name of Leisureco, started out after a pre-match conversation between two Leeds United supporters — Paul Munton and Steve McCann. They were reminiscing how wonderful the 1960's plain white Leeds shirts were and how much they would like one to sport at Elland Road games.

Gordon Strachan —modelling the Leeds United strip of the 60's.

OLD DAYS!

Glasgow Rangers — 70's.

As a result they began to have exact replicas of these shirts made and marketed them through the club fanzine, The Square Ball.

Demand was so great that they soon introduced the famous yellow away top, as worn by the likes of Peter Lorimer, Eddie and Frank Gray and Jack Charlton.

Orders flooded in and it soon became clear to the lads that all their trouble had been worthwhile. At first they had found it difficult to locate a manufacturing company with the machinery necessary to create exact replicas.

In order to be indistinguishable from those of twenty years previous, the shirts had to be made from the material of the day — cotton.

But once that hurdle had been successfully negotiated, there seemed to be nothing stopping the firm from branching out.

Contact with other clubs led to expansion and new teams were added to the Arkwright's range. Even international jerseys went into production, with England's red World Cup winning 1966 top proving popular, along with the black Russian goalkeeping shirt made famous by Lev Yashin.

Not only were kits reminiscent of the past, they were exact in every detail. Those details didn't always come from the memory banks of Arkwright employees either.

Research was undertaken to search out precise details of every garment produced. The clubs could sometimes help in this task, but otherwise it was a case of digging out relevant books to find clear pictures from which to work.

It all meant that the company could market their products knowing they were precisely the same as they were years ago. There is, however, one slight difference. The embroidery of badges is of a better quality because of the advances in textile machinery.

Production also posed occasional problems. Dyeing the cotton, for example. Often, sleeves had to be dyed separately from the main body before being sewn back together. It was awkward, but just added further to the home-made feel which has proved so popular with customers.

Being cotton, the shirts are heavier and warmer than the flimsy modern day kits that are so popular, so making them a regular sight on the terraces and around the stands of our football grounds.

It's interesting that Manchester United's green and yellow jersey and the long shorts sported by so many clubs today came onto the scene after Arkwright first exploited the past. It will now be similarly interesting to see if more clubs go back to their roots for new designs.

WIN A SUPER "Arkwright" SHIRT!

SIMPLY ANSWER THE QUESTIONS BELOW AND A 50's, 60's or 70's SHIRT COULD BE YOURS!

1. Which English club did Rangers' Ally McCoist play for?

2. Manchester United won the first ever Premier League Championship. In which season did they last win the First Division title?

3. Who were the beaten finalists in last season's European Cup?

THE READERS WITH THE FIRST 10 CORRECT ENTRIES WILL WIN AN ARKWRIGHT SHIRT OF THEIR OWN CHOICE.

Arkwright Competition, Topical Times Football Book, P.O. BOX 305, LONDON NW1 1TX.

REMEMBER TO INCLUDE YOUR FULL NAME AND ADDRESS.

Please send an S.A.E. if you want a list of the prizewinners and the correct answers.

Closing date — 15th February, 1994.

HIGH KICKER

Hearts' Alan McLaren takes to the air to clear from Kevin McAllister, Falkirk

FLYING HIGH!

That's John Scales, Wimbledon, as he beats Nigel Clough, Liverpool, to the ball.

RESTORATION WORK!

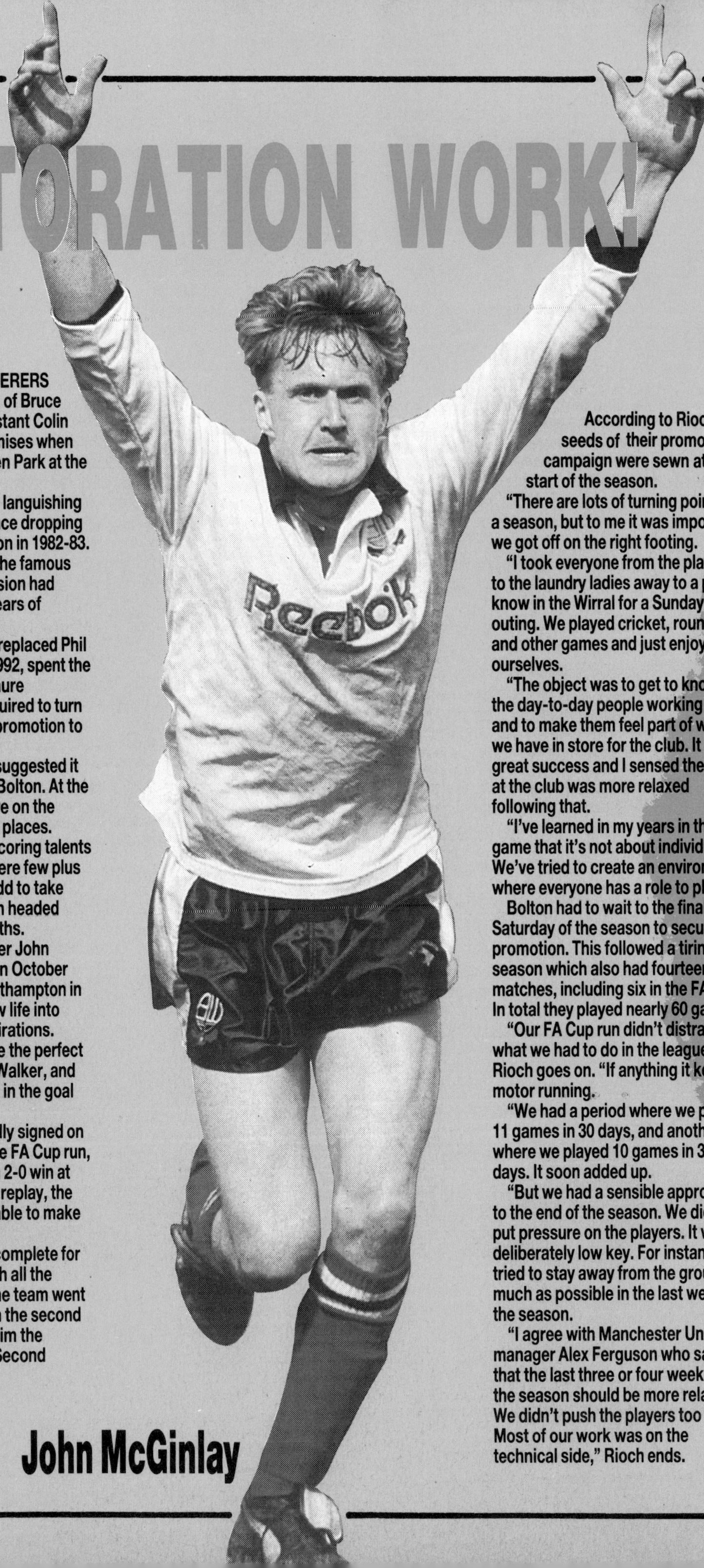

THE BOLTON WANDERERS management team of Bruce Rioch and his assistant Colin Todd made no rash promises when they took over at Burnden Park at the start of last season.

The Trotters had been languishing in the lower divisions since dropping out of the Second Division in 1982-83. It seemed that much of the famous old club's pride and passion had been drained away by years of mediocrity.

Rioch and Todd, who replaced Phil Neal in the summer of 1992, spent the early months of their tenure assessing what was required to turn the club round and win promotion to the First Division.

Early-season results suggested it would be a struggle for Bolton. At the end of October they were on the fringes of the relegation places. Apart from the prolific scoring talents of Andy Walker, there were few plus points for Rioch and Todd to take comfort in as the season headed towards the winter months.

But the arrival of striker John McGinlay from Millwall in October and David Lee from Southampton in November breathed new life into Bolton's promotion aspirations.

McGinlay proved to be the perfect partner for fellow Scot Walker, and was soon matching him in the goal stakes.

Winger Lee was initially signed on loan, but after a lucrative FA Cup run, which included a dream 2-0 win at Anfield in a third Round replay, the money was made available to make the signing permanent.

The jigsaw was now complete for Rioch and Todd and with all the pieces neatly in place the team went on an impressive rally in the second half of the season to claim the runners-up spot in the Second Division.

According to Rioch, the seeds of their promotion campaign were sewn at the start of the season.

"There are lots of turning points in a season, but to me it was important we got off on the right footing.

"I took everyone from the players to the laundry ladies away to a place I know in the Wirral for a Sunday outing. We played cricket, rounders and other games and just enjoyed ourselves.

"The object was to get to know all the day-to-day people working here and to make them feel part of what we have in store for the club. It was a great success and I sensed the mood at the club was more relaxed following that.

"I've learned in my years in the game that it's not about individuals. We've tried to create an environment where everyone has a role to play."

Bolton had to wait to the final Saturday of the season to secure promotion. This followed a tiring season which also had fourteen cup matches, including six in the FA Cup. In total they played nearly 60 games.

"Our FA Cup run didn't distract what we had to do in the league," Rioch goes on. "If anything it kept the motor running.

"We had a period where we played 11 games in 30 days, and another where we played 10 games in 30 days. It soon added up.

"But we had a sensible approach to the end of the season. We didn't put pressure on the players. It was deliberately low key. For instance, I tried to stay away from the ground as much as possible in the last week of the season.

"I agree with Manchester United's manager Alex Ferguson who said that the last three or four weeks of the season should be more relaxing. We didn't push the players too much. Most of our work was on the technical side," Rioch ends.

John McGinlay

Centimetre SOCCER

ANOTHER World Cup football tournament will take place in 1994. Qualifying tournaments have been held all over the world, and organisers have been busy checking out facilities for the final stages.

Officials and participants will stay in top hotels — but the players will be housed and transported in small boxes!

For this is the Subbuteo World Cup, the table-top version of football's major tournament. And just like the real thing this championship is becoming big business.

Sponsorship deals, commercial marketing, television coverage, the lot. There is even an attempt to get Subbuteo accepted for the Olympic Games!

The world's top finger-flickers are warming up for '94. National champions from over 30 countries are likely to contest the final stages of the World Cup.

The Russians are sending a contestant for the first time, and there will be an inaugural individual Women's Championship.

Subbuteo is played by over 5 million people in more than 50 countries worldwide. The English factory will produce around 15 million figures this year.

Around 800 different teams are available in the range, including club and international sides, all in authentic 'strips'.

The game is about 60 years old, although it was first marketed to the public in 1947. The figures were made of cardboard, and there were no accessories.

The original set had no playing pitch — just a piece of chalk and instructions to mark out the pitch on an old ex-army blanket.

The game has grown steadily ever since those early days. There are now more than 400 Subbuteo Clubs and leagues in Britain alone.

Twenty-five countries took part in the last World Cup in 1990. Shadowing the real thing, the Subbuteo World Cup final was held in Rome — but the winner was from Greece, not Germany.

The World Cup in 1994 is being organised by the newly formed Federation of International Subbuteo Table Football. The FISTF was founded during the European Championships in 1992, with the aim of establishing Subbuteo as a world sport.

The Federation immediately applied to the International Olympic Committee in a bid to be accepted for the Olympic Games.

Not bad for a sport in which the players are only 2 cms tall!

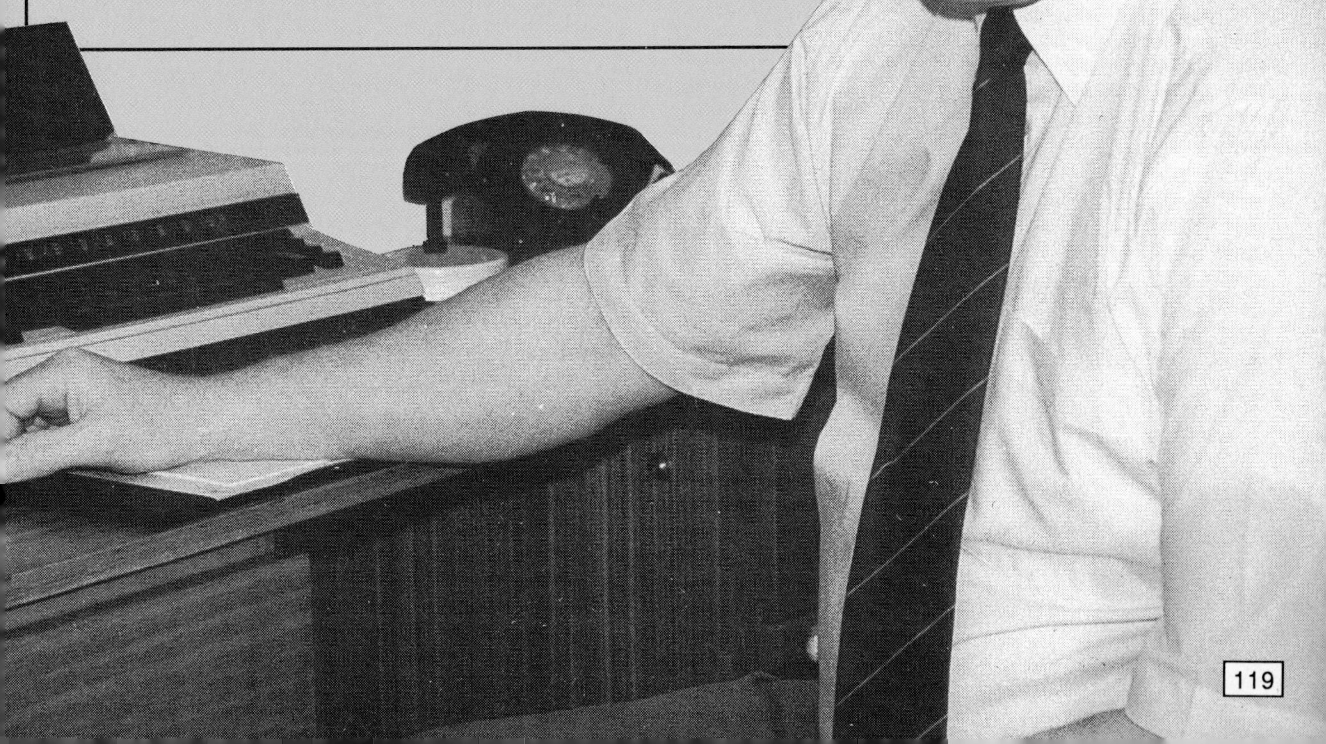

Scottish Regional Subbuteo Organiser, Bob McGiffen. Bob is a past Scottish champion but now specialises in refereeing, and will be on duty at the World Cup Finals. Bob's spare time is almost all devoted to the sport, travelling all over Europe publicising, promoting, organising and refereeing table soccer.

Alex Ferguson's recipe for Championship success at Old Trafford had two vital ingredients, says Manchester United's MARK HUGHES . . .

FRENCH POLISH!

THE ARRIVAL of Eric Cantona from Leeds United in early December turned out to be the most significant signing of last season.

When he joined Manchester United from reigning First Division champions Leeds United it caused a storm of controversy on both sides of the Pennines.

Leeds fans were unhappy to see the classy Frenchman leave Elland Road, and many Manchester United fans wondered if his style of play would suit the Old Trafford side's system.

As it turns out, the sceptical Manchester fans need not have worried. Cantona pepped up Manchester United's Championship challenge which had shown signs of faltering before his arrival.

It also took a hefty weight off Mark Hughes' shoulders. The Welshman admits Cantona's signing breathed new life into his own game.

The 30-year-old striker explains, "For the majority of last season and the start of this I was playing upfront on my own.

"I had to turn my back to goal and try to hold the ball up to wait for support coming from midfield. I was often up against it and heavily marked.

"It was difficult to impose myself on the game at times because I wasn't able to get freedom to pick the ball up in space and run at defences as often as I'd have liked.

"Eric coming has made a big difference to me. We are able to share the workload and that's taken a lot of pressure off me.

"He has great ball control, and can shield the ball very well. That gives me time to find space and his distribution is superb.

"I've not scored as many goals as I'd have liked since Eric's arrival, but I'm the club's top scorer for the first time in a few years and that's particularly pleasing.

"I'm also pleased with my over-all game. My contribution in other departments of the game is far more consistent. Eric has a lot to do with that."

SINCE the days of George Best at Manchester United there has been no shortage of young players who have been groomed as a likely successor to the former wing wizard.

Sadly, until now there hasn't really been a player who has come close to recreating the silky magic of Best.

But Ryan Giggs has caused understandable excitement at Old Trafford. His performances since breaking into the first team a couple of seasons ago have even got Best raving about him.

It seems that United at last have found someone who can perform the role which Best fulfilled during United's glory days of the 1960s.

Mark Hughes admits that Giggs' meteoric rise to being a United and Wales regular has been hugely impressive.

THE SECOND BEST!

"It's amazing to think what he has achieved in such a short space of time," Hughes says. "Two Young Player of the Year awards, a United regular and several Wales caps.

"When I was 19, I was still stuck in United's reserves waiting to break into the first team.

"We all know Ryan's ability, but it's the way he conducts himself which has caught my eye. He takes everything in his stride.

"His reputation is such that there is always so much expected of him when he takes the field. But he seems to cope without any problems at all. I know it isn't easy with all the pressure put on a player at a young age.

"I think kids nowadays are given a first-team chance more quickly than when I was starting out. I had to wait for injuries and suspensions before I could get a foot in the door.

"Managers seem to be more prepared to take chances. They work on the principle: 'If you're good enough, you're old enough.'

"When I first came into the United team I was in awe of many of my team-mates. I used to sit in the dressing room and keep pinching myself. Looking at Ryan, I don't think he's in awe of any of us.

"He may seem a quiet lad, but I can assure you he's not shy or naive. He's very street-wise and copes very well with the dressing-room banter.

"I often offer him advice and I like to think he's taken some of it on board. But most of the time he doesn't need help from me. Sometimes I think he can teach me a thing or two."

Hughes believes Giggs is set for a long future at international level as well as at club level for United.

"He just seems to carry on with Wales where he left off with United."

MR

IN the battle of the goalkeepers, two men dominated the English scene last season — Chris Woods of Sheffield Wednesday and David Seaman of Arsenal.

Between them, those two not only carved up the international arena. They also hogged the spotlight in the showpiece matches at domestic level.

In the end, honours were even. Woods went through the campaign as the England number one goalkeeper.

At club level, however, Seaman had the upper hand as the two clubs contested both major finals.

In a remarkable trilogy of Wembley confrontations between the sides from London and Yorkshire, the teams first met in the Coca-Cola Cup Final, with Arsenal coming out on top with a 2-1 victory in extra time.

A month later, they were back for the FA Cup Final and, following stalemate at the first attempt, it was Arsenal again who lifted the trophy in most dramatic fashion.

As they braced themselves for the first ever penalty shoot-out in an FA Cup Final, the Gunners nicked it in the last minute of extra time, defender Andy Linighan's powerful header reaching the net with the aid of an unfortunate fumble by Woods.

But if the Wednesday 'keeper was distraught over his part in the deciding goal, his composure was quickly regained as he prepared for the ultimately disastrous end-of-season trips to Poland and Norway, where Woods shouldered part of the blame as England dropped three vital World Cup qualifying points.

Putting his troubles behind him, however, is simply a natural part of Woods' make-up. The 'Mr Cool' of football, he is the epitomy of composure and lives for the big-game atmosphere. Nothing ruffles him.

Says Chris, "I have always been very calm and quiet, and take everything in my stride. It is just my natural attitude.

"There have been plenty of matches throughout my career when things have become a bit hectic, but I take the view that there is no point in flying off the handle or letting myself get flustered. I just get on with the job."

That even temperament was amply illustrated last season when England came under bombardment from an evil mob of Turkish fans as they won a World Cup qualifying match 2-0 in Izmir.

Woods was struck on the shoulder by a coin as missiles rained all around him but, typical of his unflappability, he let the incident pass without fuss.

"I just shrugged it off and thought no more about it as I concentrated all my thoughts on the match," he recalls. "To be honest, I did not even notice the intimidating atmosphere which everybody told me about afterwards. I simply wasn't aware of it."

In fact, acclimatisation to the big occasion was completed early in his career when, as a raw 18-year-old, he turned out in a League Cup Final for Nottingham Forest at Wembley, the venue which has virtually become his second home.

That season, 1977-78, he was the understudy to Peter Shilton at the City Ground, and did not play a single League match. However, Shilton was cup-tied in the League Cup, so for that competition only, Woods was handed the first-team jersey.

After going all the way to the final, the youngster kept out a Liverpool side which included Kenny Dalglish, Terry McDermott, Ian Callaghan and Steve Heighway. Following a 0-0 draw at Wembley, Forest won the replay at Old Trafford by a John Robertson penalty.

"I think that final had a

COOL

That's SHEFFIELD WEDNESDAY'S CHRIS WOODS.

big influence on my ability to remain calm no matter what is happening around me," Chris goes on.

"The Wembley match in particular was such a big, potentially nerve-wracking occasion, especially for somebody so young and inexperienced. If I had let it, I suppose the occasion might have become too much for me.

"I had heard some of the Liverpool players talking beforehand about their first appearances at Wembley and how they hadn't produced their best form because they had been awestruck.

"I set out to make sure that would not happen to me. When I walked out on to the pitch before the game, I completely took in the atmosphere and went on to enjoy the whole afternoon. I believe that experience has stood me in good stead for the rest of my career. I have been able to approach every game in a totally relaxed frame of mind."

In order to make sure he stays that way, however, Woods ensures that his mental preparation for games is always correct. For him, that means spending several hours each week in a sauna, sweating away his worries.

Several times a week, he disappears on his own to sit for an hour or so, alone with his thoughts in the steaming-hot, yet relaxing, atmosphere.

It has become such an important ritual that Chris even had a sauna installed in his home.

"I love it," he enthuses. "I go in there all the time because I find it such an ideal way to relax. For perhaps an hour, I can just wash away my pressures and strains.

"I generally sit in the steam room for about 15 minutes, then take a cold bath before going back for another session. When I'm away on a football trip, the hotel we stay in often has a sauna, so I make full use of that, too.

"I just sit and think about things, whether it is football or everyday issues. If I have any problems, it is a perfect way to work them out and get them out of my system.

"For a goalkeeper, it is so important to get your mental preparations right before a match. I do all my physical work during the week in training, but I don't have a lot of physical work on a Saturday. Most of my business during a match is about staying alert, so mental toughness is important. The sauna helps to give me that."

Another important part of Woods' preparation takes place on the training field and by playing outfield and banging in a few goals!

During practice, he has become a regular goalscorer, and reports that his avoidance of playing between the posts has been of crucial benefit to him.

"I don't think it does a 'keeper any harm to have a taste of playing outfield during the week, especially since the new pass-back rule came into effect," he explains.

"In fact, I have been playing outfield in training for a number of years now. It is a legacy from my early days when we used to play five-a-side games using small goals.

"In my opinion it was a bad thing for a goalkeeper to have to get used to covering such a small area, then have to deal with a full-size goal in matches.

"In addition, when you are defending a small net, it is usual to react to an opponent bearing down on you by falling down in front of him. When applied to normal-sized nets, this again breeds bad habits.

"Fortunately, all my clubs have agreed with me and allowed me to play outfield on training days. I also do that when I am with the England squad.

"It also helps me to keep fit and busy. When you are standing around between the posts in a practice match, you tend to become stiff. But I enjoy getting out there and having a good runaround. I get up a good sweat and by the time we are finished I feel that I have had a good work-out. Afterwards, I do my own specialist goalkeeping work, so that is never neglected.

"The benefits, however, have been even more evident during the past year or so. The pass-back rule, when it was introduced last season, has meant that 'keepers have had to become more like sweepers and have the ball at their feet more often. So the more I play outfield, the more comfortable I feel on the ball."

Wembley woe! Last season's F.A. Cup Final replay, and Woods is beaten by Andy Linighan's last-minute header.

PETER SCHMEICHEL
Manchester United

YOUR PICTURE GUIDE

ACTION! COLOUR!

PIN-UPS!

Printed and Published in Great Britain by D.C. THOMSON & CO. LTD., 185 Fleet Street, London EC4A 2HS.

ISBN 0-85116-561-3

SCOTTISH First Division Cowdenbeath set one record after another last season — all for the wrong reasons. A run of 30 games without a win and losing over 100 goals during the season saw them relegated weeks before the end of the season. And to make matters worse, part of their stand burnt down!

Goalmouth action v. Ayr United. Cowdenbeath failed to win a home match throughout season 92-93 — another unhappy statistic.

Central Park, Cowdenbeath, capacity 4778. Over 25,000 crammed in here to see Rangers, back in 1949. Now, home gates average only 300.